Print & Pattern
Bowie Style

LAURENCE KING

Published in 2010 by
Laurence King Publishing Ltd
361–373 City Road
London EC1V 1LR
United Kingdom
Tel: +44 20 7841 6900
Fax: +44 20 7841 6910
e-mail: enquiries@laurenceking.com

www.laurenceking.com

A catalogue record for this book is
available from the British Library.

ISBN 978-1-85669-646-3

Book and cover design: & SMITH
www.andsmithdesign.com
Senior Editor: Peter Jones
Printed in China.

Endpapers: Sanna Annukka

Print &
Pattern

Bowie Style

Laurence King Publishing

Contents

Introduction

Marie Perkins

a.k.a. Bowie Style

www.printpattern.blogspot.com

Mention to someone that you are a surface pattern designer and you will probably receive a blank look of confusion. Perhaps they will hear the word 'pattern' and think you design patterns for clothing, or that by 'surface' you are referring to the different types of finish used in building and decorating trades. Either way, they won't realize you are a graphic designer, illustrator, textile designer and more, all rolled into one. Pretty much anything you see in the marketplace that has a printed design on it will have been through the hands of a surface designer. The plates you eat from, the fabric of your tablecloth, the design on your rug, your curtains, wallpaper, cushions, handbags, wrapping paper, birthday card, and so much more, any product with a surface print or pattern on it is part of this often overlooked form of design.

When I first began to use the internet as a research tool for my job as a designer, I could find no website or blog dedicated solely to surface design, instead they seemed always to include furniture, fashion and three-dimensional design in between the bits that interested me. So I decided to create my own site, called Print & Pattern, in my spare time, and started to share my research with readers. Not many at first, but gradually word got out and eventually hits were counted in millions. Graduates and designers asked to appear on the site to showcase themselves to the many companies that were using it to recruit fresh talent, while I scoured the shops with my trusty spy camera and exposed the exciting design that could be found in London, Paris and New York. Designs are now placed up on the site to be admired and celebrated, as well as to help keep an eye on trends.

When I signed up to the blog software I decided to use a pseudonym, to remain anonymous, and glanced around the room for an idea. I had a new book at the time, about my hero David Bowie, called *Bowie Style*, and thought that would do nicely. Little did I know several years later that the name Bowie would stick.

Soon the love and enthusiasm I have for pattern design was spotted by Laurence King Publishing, who asked if I would like to compile a book on the subject. As a collector of design books, naturally I jumped at the chance to curate my own. And so, here is a selection of works by fabulous designers from all over the world, united by a love of the printed pattern.

Absolute Zero Degrees

www.absolutezerodegrees.com
www.minimoderns.com
keith@absolutezerodegrees.com

01 //   Absolute Zero Degrees is a London-based design and branding agency created by graphic designers Keith Stephenson and Mark Hampshire. They also have their own collection of designer products, and have produced wallpaper, ceramics and fabrics. In 2006 they launched the new brand 'Mini Moderns', for their collection of contemporary designs for children.

Top / Net and Ball
The Southbank Centre asked Keith and Mark to redraw the classic design by Peter Moro and Leslie Martin, the architects of the Royal Festival Hall. They changed the proportions to a much more workable and commercial scale for wallpaper, and introduced a new collection of colours to create a soft, modernist palette.

Below / Town Square
A fabric designed for a 'Mini Moderns' floor cushion. Architectural drawings of buildings and trees populate the pattern which uses a grid layout.

Tick-Tock is one of Absolute Zero Degrees' 'Colour-Me' wallpapers, designed to be coloured in, once on the wall. Twelve clocks of varying styles, all set at different times, help children to learn to tell the time in a relaxed and fun way.

Above / Bees
This wallpaper, created for 'Places and Spaces', features a central
honeycomb structure that morphs into bees and butterflies.
The designers wanted the print to feel like a cameo brooch or
a rococo mirror, so used the oval shape as a negative space.

Top / Dandelions
Created for 'Places and Spaces',
the large dandelion clock
on this wallpaper explodes to
form dragonflies.

Far left / Sitting Comfortably?
A cushion from the 'Mini
Moderns' collection. "Are you
sitting comfortably?" is a
phrase that usually precludes
a great story.

Left / Tick-Tock Cushion
The 'Mini Moderns' floor
cushion has crossover appeal
to both children and adults.

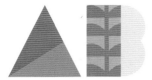

Alice Burrows

www.aliceapple.co.uk
aliceeburrows@yahoo.co.uk

02 // Alice Burrows, also known as Alice Apple, is based in the south Devon coastal town of Teignmouth. Alice's main influences include fabrics from the '60s, vintage Scandinavian textiles and retro fabrics from Japan. Alice enjoys sewing and makes toys and accessories with vintage and retro fabrics, and her designs are also featured on various homewares.

Top / Birds and Flowers
The flower and fruit shapes are inspired by the strong imagery of Scandinavian textiles of the 1960s. The birds add a sense of playfulness.

Bottom / Coffee Pot
This motif was inspired by Alice's own collection of vintage coffee pots.

Opposite / Swedish Flower Mix
Alice had stationery in mind when she created this fun floral image, influenced by Orla Kiely. She has since applied the design in her own shop to mugs, coasters, posters and more.

Opposite / Pear Bird
Alice found inspiration for this design in the inks supplied by a Japanese gocco company which come in beautiful, strong, matte colours.

Above / Apple Bird Banner
A Japanese card-printing machine is used to print this greetings card. Classic retro-shaped flowers in Scandinavian colours form part of Alice's brand identity.

Allison Cole

www.allisoncoleillustration.com
www.bangbangyourethread.com
allison@allisoncoleillustration.com

03 // Allison Cole is based in
Providence, Rhode Island. A graduate
of the Rhode Island School of
Design, Allison fell in love with
the art of hand-made multiples as a
Printmaking major. Since then she
has made her living as a freelance
illustrator, creating a variety of art,
from digital design to paper-cut prints
and sewn objects that she exhibits in
galleries and at craft shows, and has
sold to various retailers.

TREE NOTEBOOK
100 blank pages

Opposite / Christmas
This Christmas tree design
uses non-traditional colours
and tiny geometric patterns
to create a highly
contemporary look.

Above / Tree
Stationery design for
Bang Bang You're Thread
designed to spread an
environmental message.

Top left / Tree Pattern
A variety in the shapes of the
trees used gives this surface
design real interest. The
key colour, like the message
intended, is green.

Left / Cloud Pattern
The theme for this pattern
is 'come rain or shine' and
features a cute, happy cloud in
the sun and a sad one in the
rain. Surface design for Bang
Bang You're Thread.

Amanda Dilworth

www.amandadilworth.co.uk
amanda.dilworth1@btinternet.com

04 // Amanda Dilworth is a freelance designer with a BA in Surface Pattern Design. Her studio is situated on the outskirts of the beautiful Derbyshire Dales, from where she draws a great deal of her inspiration. Amanda's designs are contemporary with a strong illustrative feel, and she enjoys using a combination of pattern and illustration within her work. Amanda uses both traditional and digital techniques, and has a substantial amount of work published within the greetings card and stationery markets.

Above / Bees
A fondness for the busy
bumble-bee inspired this
design, after Amanda read
about the diminishing bee
population. Amanda believes
that these under-appreciated
little workers deserve to be
recognized for the incredibly
important job they do as
the vital pollinators to our
food chain.

Left / Floral 3
This design was inspired
by the amazing English
countryside, where wild
flowers and grasses create
carpets of beautiful colours
and patterns.

Amanda Luke Designs

www.amandalukedesigns.co.uk
info@amandalukedesigns.co.uk

05 // Amanda Luke is a freelance surface pattern designer based in the UK, with work that sells internationally. Working mainly in digital format, with some hand-painted artwork, she designs for womenswear, stationery and wrapping papers, although creating childrenswear is what inspires Amanda most, because of its fun and naive quality.

Above / Ladybird and Friends
Created in Photoshop for use in children's wear or stationery, inspired by vintage and retro images.

Opposite / Spotty Bird
This quirky design, created using Photoshop, featuring birds and flowers was aimed at the children's wear and stationery market.

Amy Cartwright

www.amycartwright.com
mail@amycartwright.com

06 // Amy Cartwright is based in Illinois, and trained at Central Saint Martins in London, where she studied Illustration and Graphic Design. Amy loves to travel, and uses her explorations to inspire her work, which has been picked up by various well-known clients.

Top / Fluffy Mouse
Amy created this cute little mouse to be the identity picture on her blog.

Bottom / Stickers
Digital, self-promotional stickers designed as a cute promo piece that would have a further fun use for the recipient.

Top / Peacock
The peacock is the most decorative of birds and it is beautifully illustrated here in muted colours with sketchy lines. The design was created for a greetings card.

Bottom / Dog Walk Dog
Amy wanted to create a little story which was told as it wrapped around the mug. The mug was part of a series given out as holiday gifts.

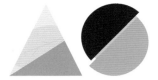

Amy Schimler

www.amyschimler.com
www.redfishcircle.blogspot.com
amy@amyschimler.com

07 // Amy Schimler is a freelance illustrator and surface pattern designer working in the Atlanta area. She studied Fibre Arts and Painting in Boston, and followed up with Textile Design at Rhode Island School of Design. She sells her surface designs to the apparel and home goods market and also works as a freelance artist for American Greetings. Amy has licensed art to several companies for children's products and the quilting and home-sewing market.

Top / Birds with Flower Vases
This was one design in a series of six coordinating prints that was licensed to Robert Kaufman Fabrics and for the collection 'On a Whim'. The style of illustration is loose and sketchy with a chalky crayon effect.

Bottom / Spring Birds
Another design from the 'On a Whim' collection. Roughened edges and brush effects here give the pattern a hand-painted feel.

Opposite / Owl Toss
This was a digital piece that was purchased by American Greetings to use for stationery products. Having the owls all at different angles gives the pattern a sense of movement.

Amy Wilde

www.amywilde.co.uk
amy_wilde@hotmail.com

o8//   Amy Wilde studied at the University of Teeside, where she took a degree in Graphic Design. While exhibiting at London's New Designers graduate show, Amy was offered a job at Hallmark Cards in West Yorkshire, where she has now been working for three and a half years, and loves the studio environment. Amy has worked mainly on Christmas designs, but her passion is characters, and she specializes in bright, funky kids' designs and working with typography. The designs featured here were created while Amy was on maternity leave.

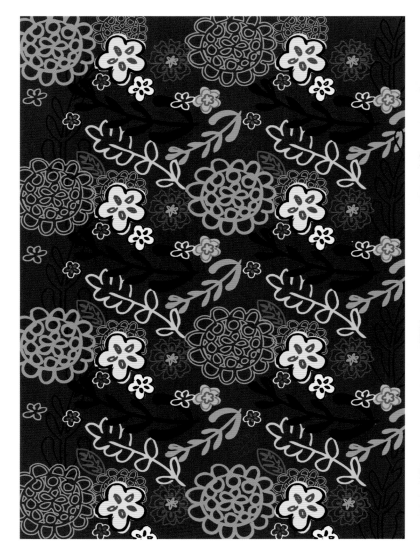

Above / Floral Dreaming
Amy filled a sketchbook with doodles of abstract flowers and shapes, then scanned them and recoloured them into a rich autumnal palette.

Opposite / Flora and Friends
The contrast between a cute graphic character and a hand-drawn pattern adds a softness to this piece.

Ana Ventura

www.anaventura.com
papeisportodolado@gmail.com

09 // Ana Ventura is a freelance designer from Portugal. She studied at the Fine Arts Faculty of the University of Lisbon, and has been involved in solo and collective shows since 1996. In her illustrations she uses a digital technique from scanned pieces of fabrics in order to achieve different layers of patterns. In 2006 Ana started making paper-cut illustrations and created a very successful range of paper dolls, which now sell all over the world.

Top / Winter Bear
Originally created digitally using Photoshop and later screenprinted, this design aims to capture the feel of Christmas and winter. From the 'Winter Days' series of illustrations. The limited edition prints were for the CPS (Centro Portugues De Serigrafia).

Middle & Bottom /
Red Riding Wood & The Little Shepherd
Inspired by the classic children's story, this design for deco tape uses graphic illustrations of highly stylised trees in a dark colour palette.

Opposite / A Little Bird on My Pocket
Ana used a digital technique from scanned pieces of fabrics in order to achieve different layers of patterns. From the 'Winter Days' series of illustrations.

Andrew Pavitt

www.andrewpavitt.com
andrewpavitt@btconnect.com

10 // Having completed a degree in Fine Art at Chelsea School of Art, Andrew Pavitt worked in a number of seemingly unrelated fields before drifting into the world of illustration. While developing both a style and a client list, he began to find increasing influence from the printed fabrics of the '50s through to the '70s, and this in turn led to a fascination with the wider applied arts in general. His love of the muted colour palette and the playful patterns used during this period formed the basis of an initial eight designs for a range of greetings cards. Now Andrew has a range of 36 designs and a loyal customer base.

Above / Night Owl
This greetings card design has a retro look, but with a contemporary approach. Inspired by the vibrant folk style and simplicity of printed textiles.

Opposite / Toikka
Greetings card design. Andrew's love of shape and form is evident in this illustration's stylised, beautifully elegant, geometric shapes.

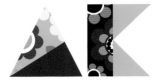

Ann Kelle Designs

www.annkelle.com
info@annkelle.com

11 //   Kelle Boyd is the founder and designer of Ann Kelle Designs. After years of working in public policy, Kelle returned to her childhood love of art, her passion rekindled when she bought art supplies as a stress reliever. Two years later, in 2006, this lead to the beginning of Ann Kelle Designs. Her colourful, fresh and modern designs now appear on a variety of paper products found on the shelves of boutiques and chain stores. Kelle says her designs are inspired "by all that we have always known and loved as kids… from dad's tie, spring flowers, ice cream, our favourite rock bands, and even the sweaters we wore in the second grade".

Top / A Victorian Tea Party
A lacy design with a nod to Victoriana and doileys. The resulting pattern is actually highly contemporary, both traditional and dramatic and new.

Bottom / A Spring Meadow
This pattern was inspired by Kelle's childhood bedroom, with walls painted Kelly green and yellow and green floral bed linen. As a child, Kelle always thought her room looked like a meadow.

Opposite / An Apple
for a Teacher
Some of Kelle's favourite people are teachers, two in particular, her mum and sister. In this design the apples are all the same shape repeated, but some are embellished with pattern to create interest.

II / Ann Kelle Designs

Opposite / From Miry Clay
Inspired by a song that "touched her soul". The flowers are simplified to become bold shapes that are almost abstract, and are held together by their stalks which give a striped layout.

Above / Spring Jazz
These flowers could conceivably be dancing around to the beat of the music.

Anna Campbell

www.lovelydaymagazine.com.au
lovelydaydesign@gmail.com

12 // Anna Campbell is based in Australia and currently working in freelance textile and surface design. Under the name Lovely Day Design, Anna takes commissions including repeat fabric designs and placement prints for fashion and homewares, as well as artwork and graphics for stationery and gift cards. Anna trained in Melbourne at RMIT University in Product Development for Fashion, and uses Illustrator to produce textile prints. Her particular areas of interest are children's textiles and illustration.

Anna is currently developing an Australian-based independent magazine for girls aged five to ten years, inspired by the storytelling and original illustrations that were prominent in childhood journals of the '50s to '70s. Anna loves all things patterned and illustrative, and is inspired by English artists Becky Blair and Rob Ryan.

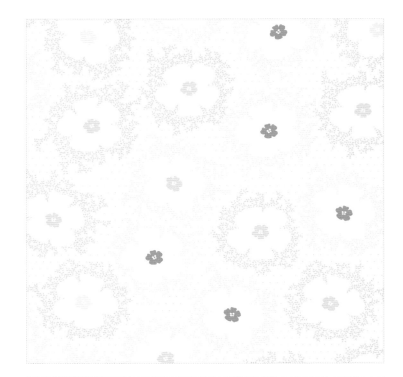

Above / Pretty Horse Print
Anna is inspired by the illustrations and designs of her childhood, as is apparent in this '70s-influenced print.

Opposite top / Petal
Anna has a passion for designing whimsical children's prints, that appeal to youngsters but also have a nostalgic attraction for adults.

Opposite bottom / Sunday
A whimsical pattern which uses flowers, birds, fruit and trees without looking too busy, using space to wonderful effect. Created for children's homeware ranges.

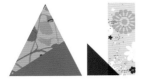

Anne Jochum

www.creabook.com/anne-jochum
anne.jochum@yahoo.fr

13 // Anne Jochum gained a master's degree in Fashion and the Environment at the Paris school of art and design Ecole Duperré. She likes to mix traditional drawing and digital techniques to create surface designs for the fashion industry, tableware, home decor, wallpaper and illustration. She has designed for Paris trend-forecasting agencies as well as for lingerie, fabrics and various companies and publications.

Top / Buttercup
Surface pattern. Hot orange spices up a neutral-coloured pattern; the random scattered dots give this design lots of movement.

Bottom / Flowers Fly
Surface pattern. A border using the same palette and motifs but with a different arrangement shows how co-ordination can be used to create collections.

Opposite / Birch Beige
Wallpaper digital print. Silhouettes layered on top of each other create an organic pattern of interesting shapes. Added texture provides some contemporary detail.

Anne Wendlandt

www.enna-online.com
enna@enna-online.com

14 //   Anne Wendlandt was born in Hanover, Germany, and has been making 'stuff' for as long as she can remember. Drawing, crafting and sewing were always her favourite activities. It was during a year spent at a high school in the US that Anne discovered graphic design, and loved the idea of having such a creative job. She went on to study Graphic Design at Hanover's University of Applied Sciences and Art, and graduated in 2005. In 2006 Anne launched her design label, enna, and opened her own shop in Hanover in 2007.

Above / Deer and Wood
As well as deer, Anne loves wood texture in graphics, and the two together make the perfect match for some fun home decor. This wall sticker is cut from vinyl that looks like wood.

Bottom / Tree Pattern
Originally designed as a background pattern for her website, Anne painted the same pattern on a wall in her shop for a forest-themed look.

Opposite / Enna Pattern
All the things Anne loves – deer, mushrooms, bunnies and whales – are united here in one pattern.

Opposite & Above /
Matryoshka
This pattern for wrapping
paper and cards is obviously
inspired by the traditional
Russian nesting dolls.
The matryoshka pattern
was Anne's first wrapping-
paper print.

Ayako Akazawa

www.lepetitgraphiste.com
info@lepetitgraphiste.com

15 // Ayako Akazawa is based
in San Francisco and works under
the name Le Petit Graphiste.
She studied graphic design at
California College of the Arts and
loves working on printed materials
such as books and stationery.
Designing patterns is her personal
passion, and Ayako would most love
to design for chocolates or textiles,
because she is passionate about
sweets and fashion.

Above / Rabbit
Ayako sketched lots of
different rabbits by hand and
picked the one that looked the
best and then re-drew it in
Illustrator. From the *Origami
Craft Pad* a product
copyrighted to Chronicle
Books LLC.

Opposite / Lawrence
Created for an *Origami Craft
Pad*, published by Chronicle
Books. Inspiration was
drawn inspiration from
old Japanese Sumi-e
(ink-and-wash painting).

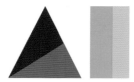

Ayelet Iontef

www.alloverprint.blogspot.com
iontef@netvision.net.il

16 // Ayelet Iontef studied Textile Design at Shenkar College of Engineering and Design in Israel. After many years working as textile designer for Kitan bed and bath, Ayelet started her own design studio, all*over*print, where she creates surface designs for home textiles and paper, and for various clients, often using hand-made drawings and paper-cuts. Ayelet also teaches at Shenkar and shares her creativity and ideas by keeping an online blog.

Right / Kaleidoscope
Hand-made paper-cuts are arranged in a composition that creates a kaleidoscope effect.

Opposite / Natasha
This design for children's bed linen was inspired by traditional Russian dolls.

BAM POP!

www.bampop.com
jj@bampop.com

17 // BAM POP! is a little design studio comprised of husband-and-wife team JJ and Jen Harrison, and based in the beautiful mountains of Utah. What began as a project to self-publish some patterned prints for use in their family scrapbooks, quickly flourished into a full line of original craft products. BAM POP! goods are now available in craft stores and gift shops all over the world. JJ graduated with highest honours from Utah Valley University, where he studied Animation and Illustration. Jen is a mother of two and a talented art director.

Top / School Supplies
A homage to their days in grade school, this design is retro, but universal at the same time, featuring items you could not live without at the time.

Middle / Die-cut Classy Frames
When creating their family scrapbooks, JJ and Jen found themselves hand drawing comic bubbles and silly frames for photos and captions, and wanted to share these elements with others.

Bottom left / Popfont 2
Numbers
Designed as a package of stamps to accessorize their school paper collection, the hand-drawn typography, with its flaws and asymmetry, complements the overall style of the line.

Bottom right / Pretty Birds
This is one of the first patterns that JJ and Jen created as a team, and their first design involving birds. Looking across their portfolio of work, you may spot a slight obsession with birds and flight.

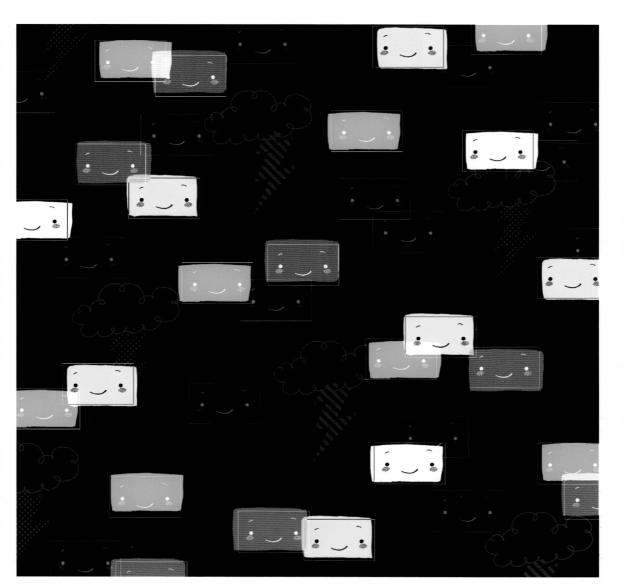

Above / 8-Bit Pop
This pattern is based on an exercise from the pair's first design classes at art school, in which the professor had students choose a piece of music and translate it into a visual pattern. They also wanted to put together a series honouring their favourite printing method, the CMYK four-colour process.

Overleaf / Ninguins
Combining two of the artists' favourite things, penguins and ninjas, every ninguin here is hand-drawn and coloured, making each one unique.

Beth Gunnell

www.bethdoodles.blogspot.com
www.theWScollection.com
beth_gunnell@btinternet.com

18 //   Beth Gunnell graduated with a BA (Hons) in Surface Decoration, and has been working as a freelance designer since 2004. She is forever doodling and gets great satisfaction from her work. She produces pieces for the worldwide greetings card market, and her designs have also been licensed for stationery, scrapbook materials and interiors. Beth also does a lot of work for childrenswear in the UK. In 2007 Beth set up a wedding stationery design and print service, The WS Collection, to provide customers with a range of fresh, contemporary designs, as well as a bespoke service.

Above / Birthday Birds
These fun birthday birds were
produced with wrapping paper
in mind. The hand-drawn detail
has been developed and finished
in Photoshop.

Left / Summer Floral
The fresh floral repeat used in
this stationery design employs
a range of colours and flower
shapes, and appeals to a wide
female age range.

Opposite / Elegant Birds
Incorporating birds into a sophisticated and elegant design results
in a contemporary pattern that would be great for stationery.

Above / Flutterby Butterfly
Pretty butterflies flutter around this design, in between decorative
paisleys and swirls. While designing in Photoshop, Beth likes to
create interest in her artwork by building up layers.

Caroline Gardner

www.carolinegardner.com
info@carolinegardner.com

19 //   Caroline Gardner, a UK-based independent greetings card designer, has enjoyed great success with her distinctive, fashion-inspired designs. Caroline trained at Chelsea College of Art and Design, and an early career as a painter gave her work a fresh, free and simple feel. Caroline Gardner Publishing was established by Caroline and her husband, Angus, and started life on the kitchen table. Before long, a buyer from John Lewis spotted the company's iconic designs – and the rest is history.

Right / Dark Moody
Flat stylised flowers are arranged on scrolling stems, thrown forwards by the darkness of the background.

Opposite top right & Opposite top left / Blue Flowers, Pink Flowers
A fresh colour palette and simple lines give these patterns a light and airy quality.

Opposite bottom /
Graphic Pattern
The flowers in this pattern are reduced to pure graphic shapes and the striking colour palette makes it stand out from the crowd.

Overleaf left /
Dark Graphic Floral
There is a hint of Japanese influence in this design. Once again dark backgrounds are used to great effect.

Overleaf right / Moody
A lighter version of the design on the right, this colour way captures all the fun of the flowers and their free-flowing movement.

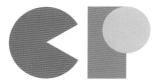

Caroline Pratt

www.carolinepratt.blogspot.com
dancinginthepark@hotmail.com

20 // Based in Leeds, printmaker and surface pattern designer Caroline Pratt finds inspiration in everything from English eccentricities and '50s textiles, to animals and contemporary illustration. With ideas taken from everyday life, and some from thin air, she produces images for various applications, including paper goods, one-off prints and books, and surface pattern. Since graduating in 2004 with a degree in Textile and Surface Pattern Design from the University of Leeds, Caroline has put her skills to good use, exhibiting in a variety of national exhibitions, selling online and through galleries, undertaking commission work for a varied client base and teaching others the art of printmaking at Leeds College of Art and Design.

Right / Owl Repeat
This repeat pattern is derived from a hand-printed book about two owls who like to sit in their tree. The lino-print motifs have been digitally coloured and manipulated in Photoshop.

heard you were feeling a
little under the weather

Happy Birthday!

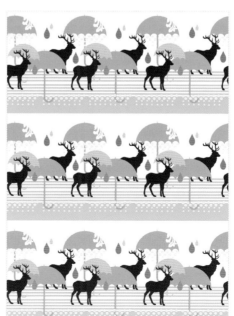

Top / Screen-printed Cards
These greetings cards have
been hand-drawn and digitally
coloured in Photoshop. A fun
colour palette is used across
all the cards, the collection
is also tied together through
the novel use of stripes.

Bottom / Stag Repeat
Derived from a hand-printed
book about a deer that gets
caught in the rain, the
lino-print motifs and
hand-drawn elements that
make up this repeat pattern
have been digitally coloured
and manipulated
in Photoshop.

Carolyn Gavin

www.ecojot.com
www.designerjots.blogspot.com
carolyngavin@rogers.com

21 // Carolyn Gavin was born and bred in Johannesburg, but has been based in Toronto for almost 19 years. She grew up in an artsy family and was having art lessons by the age of seven. She went on to study graphic design, and worked for several agencies before moving to Canada. Her family company, Mirage, introduced Ecojot in May 2007 at the National Stationery Show in New York, and it really took off from there. In May 2008, Carolyn's work was picked up by a prominent licensing agency, and her work is now being used to produce a range of fabric for the quilting industry, as well as for decorative tapes and a scrapbooking line.

Top / Owls
Fun, cheeky owls stand like cute little cupcake soldiers dressed in stylish outfits. Argyle print, spots, stripes, and more, give them a uniqueness and character.

Bottom left / Picnic and Butterflies
The butterflies have a retro, square look, while the picnic serves to bring animals together in a fun and fantastical way.

Bottom right / Apples and Owls
Ecojot produces a line of children's sketchbooks made from 100 per cent recycled materials, and want kids to be inspired by their colourful, whimsical and delicious covers.

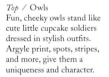

Top left / Flower Garden Rethink
One of the most popular designs in the Ecojot range, this fun pattern has a subtle but strong message that gets people thinking, and hopefully doing better, for the environment.

Bottom left / Robins Green
An Ecojot bestseller, this fresh, sweet print features lots of movement, with birds flying back and forth.

Top right / Flower Garden Aqua
A combination of flowers and veggies, this pattern is based on Carolyn's own garden, where she likes to sit a tomato plant next to a rose bush.

Bottom right / Trees and Leaves
Nature is a constant source of inspiration for Carolyn, and the variety of leaf shapes and colours to choose from is endless. She finds trees and their offspring of acorns, seeds, leaves, flowers, berries, pods and fruit really quite amazing.

Cath Kidston

www.cathkidston.co.uk
orderenquiries@cathkidston.co.uk

22 // Cath Kidston is famous for her vintage-inspired prints, which feature on everything from clothing and accessories to a variety of homewares and home furnishings. Through her designs she gives classic prints a refreshingly modern edge. Cath opened her first shop in Notting Hill in 1993, selling old furniture and vintage fabrics, a venture that soon led her to create her own distinctive fabric and product designs. There are now 21 shops in the UK, and her style has a cult following of loyal customers in Japan, where there are now three stores. Cath Kidston is continually involved in every aspect of the business, and she is both designer and creative director.

Right / Bubble Rose
Roses are a signature print for Cath Kidston, and new variations are created each season. This one takes a fresh, modern approach, and is used on everything from bed linen to brollies.

Top / Pop Flowers Red
This fun floral design,
inspired by '70s pop prints,
is available in a variety of
different colour-ways.

Bottom / Breakfast
A cheerful breakfast print
perfect for the kitchen,
this design features on
cotton, oilcloth and a range
of kitchen accessories.

Chyanne Ganzel

www.chyanneganzel.com
hello@chyanneganzel.com

23 // Chyanne Ganzel studied Communication Design at Milwaukee Institute of Art and Design, and the patterns shown here are just five from a series that she created as part of her thesis project, investigating colour and its psychological relation to personality types. Chyanne examined why people are attracted to one colour more than another, and what that attraction says about an individual's personality. The colours were then applied to pattern designs for wrapping paper and stationery, to serve as a gift of personal knowledge and fun.

Right / Yellow
Adjectives- social, expressive, leader, opinionated, wise, precise, cheerful, humorous.

Opposite top left / Blue
Adjectives - honest, thoughtful, logical, self-controlled, calm, cautious, passive, patient.

Opposite top right / Green
Adjectives - well balanced, gentle, sincere, friendly, natural, hopeful, benevolent, a minimalist.

Opposite bottom left / Red
Adjectives - ambitious, energetic, outgoing, passionate, strong, aggressive, impulsive, courageous.

Opposite bottom right / Orange
Adjectives - unique, social, friendly, curious, down-to-earth, active outdoors, restless but organized.

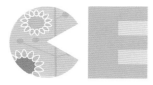

Claire Ebdy

maggie2007@gmx.com

24 // Claire Ebdy is a freelance children's print designer based in Dalton-in-Furness in Cumbria. Claire obtained a BA (Hons) in textiles and surface design at Cleveland College of Art and Design. She loves working in Illustrator and Photoshop, and also enjoys using fabrics and other tactile materials. Claire is very versatile, and finds wildlife and the environment a great inspiration.

Top / Bird in a Tree
Claire enjoys using wildlife in her work, and this, one of her simplest designs, was created very quickly one morning.

Bottom / Woodland Creatures
In this design, created while Claire was teaching herself Illustrator, cute characters inhabit a brightly coloured wood. A stitching effect has been used to add to the playful design.

Opposite / Friendship Scroll
Produced in Illustrator, this design is child-like, yet still with a great amount of detail.

Clare Nicolson

www.clarenicolson.com
info@clarenicolson.com

25 // Clare Nicolson is a textile designer based in Scotland. Her work combines digitally printed cottons and silks with vintage fabric to create a fresh range of interior textiles and accessories. Clare works from her home studio creating a wide range of products that sell in stores worldwide, as well as undertaking freelance work for many design companies. Her designs are taken from paper collages created using decorative papers and packaging.

Top / Lovey Dovey
Middle / Birds
Bottom / Pretty Peacock
A series of stylised birds created from paper and vintage pieces was digitally printed onto cushions of either cotton or silk. All the birds have a pattern or texture inside their shape to create interest.

Opposite / Milky
Created for a digitally printed teatowel, Clare's collage is applied as a printed appliqué. Graph paper has been used to create the milk bottle and flowers have been layered on top.

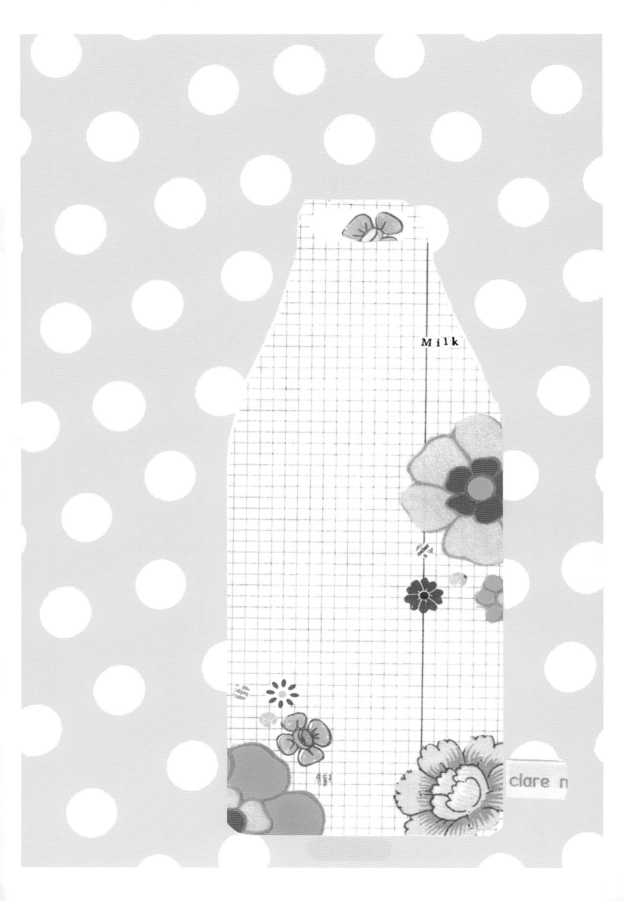

Milk

clare n

Above / Christmas Olga
Top right / Olga
A unique modern version of a
traditional Russian Matryoshka
provided the inspiration for
these illustrations designed
for use on greetings cards.

Opposite / Secret Garden
A carefully crafted collage
has been put together from
illustrations and vintage
papers to create a beautiful
new design.

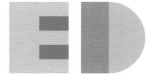

Ella Doran

www.elladoran.co.uk
ella@elladoran.co.uk

26 // Ella Doran is well known
for her photographic homewares.
Tablemats, coasters, roller blinds and
tableware all become blank canvases
for her innovative use of photographs,
featuring themes from nature and the
world around us. Ella received a
Prince's Trust loan in 1996, allowing
her to exhibit her first range of
tablemats at the UK trade show
Top Drawer, where she won Highly
Commended Best New Product for
her 'Stones' collection, a design that
set the trend for photographic
imagery on homeware products.
Since then Ella has gone on to
win awards and work with a variety
of clients.

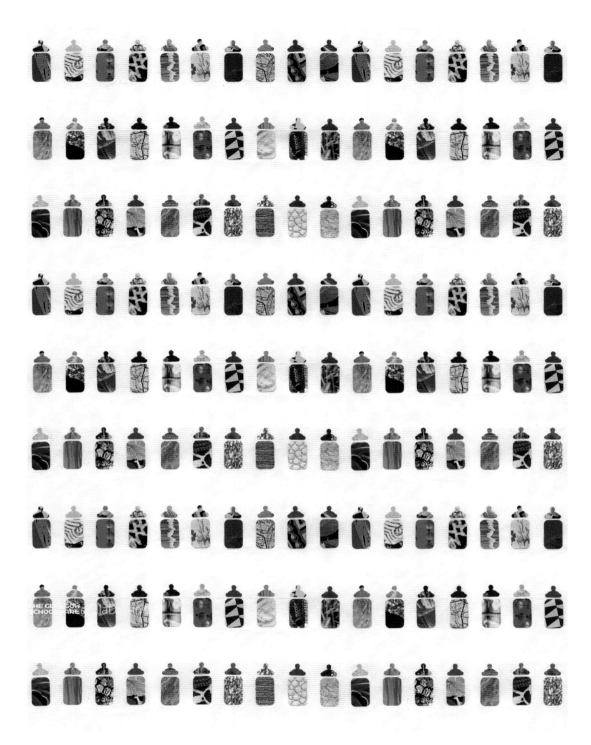

Opposite / Hearts
Each multi-coloured heart on this pattern, exclusively
produced for department store John Lewis, displays an
individual photograph.

Above / Bottles
This wrapping paper was again exclusively produced for John
Lewis, and features individual photographs cut into the shape
of cute baby bottles.

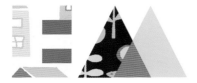

Erin McMorris

www.erinmc.com
erin@erinmc.com

27 // Erin McMorris is a freelance designer based in Portland, Oregon. She studied Graphic Design at the University of Cincinnati, followed by Textile Design at the Fashion Institute of Technology in New York City. Erin has worked in London, San Francisco and New York, designing graphic, fun, contemporary prints for a variety of products, including bedding, women's and children's apparel, paper products and towels. Although Erin draws everything on the computer, she aims to retain a hand-drawn look within her work.

Right / Poppy Dot Floral
Part of Erin's 'Park Slope' collection for FreeSpirit Fabric, she held on to for years until she finally had the opportunity to have it printed onto fabric. The whimsical floral print is given a more dramatic edge through the use of the stunning dark background. It throws the flowers forwards, giving them a luminous quality.

Opposite top / Tree Line
The trees in this pattern, pared down to the most simple shapes and arranged in a striped repeat, have an almost psychedelic look. Originally created for greetings cards.

Opposite bottom / Houses
Architecture has always provided inspiration to the designer and recently there has been a trend towards little villages and houses. Here the random colourful houses at the top contrast perfectly with the geometry of the simple linear houses below.

Fifi Mandirac

www.fifimandirac.com
fifi@fifimandirac.com

28 // Fifi Mandirac started her graphic design company eight years ago. At first she worked mainly on wedding and birth announcements, but the business soon grew and Fifi began designing cards for many occasions. Now Fifi likes to work with anything that can take a colourful design, including notebooks, bags and fans. Fifi occasionally works on commissions for other companies, and is based in Saint-Denis, near Paris, in a studio full of light in the back of her garden, which she finds very inspiring.

Right / Marouschkas
These are a family that grow with the years. The first one was designed in 2001, the latest one just this summer. Playful colours and cute faces add to their charm.

Opposite top / Fleurs Pop!
A bold retro flower shape has been filled with colourful centres for use on notebooks.

Opposite bottom / Anenomes
Another graphic floral pattern, but this time using black centres to create a more sombre design for cards.

Top / Badges
Beautiful patterned badges
are stylishly mounted.
The background patterns are
muted compared to those of
the bold badges, and playful
typography completes the effect.

Middle / Envelopes Canaris
A lighthearted, fun design
featuring canaries, where
uniquely the cloud is the line
for writing the address.

Bottom / Fleurs d'Annette
Modern graphic flowers on
long leafy stems create a design
for a card that rolls up on itself
to become a little lantern.

Opposite top / Daisy Bleue
The daisy is one of the simplest
flowers and keeping it to a
simple repeat makes this design
very easy on the eye. Several
colour-ways are used on cards,
but here the red and blue look
fabulous together when
separated by white.

Opposite bottom / 32 Père Noel
and Fleur Noel
Fifi has created a cute Father
Christmas character where his
hat and beard become geometric
shapes that can be played with
to form patterns. Part of a
collection of Christmas cards.

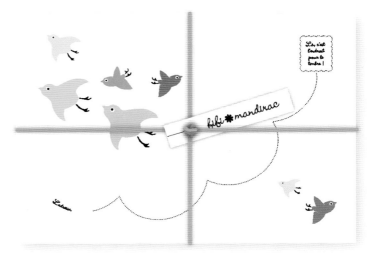

FlipFlopDesign

http://flipflopdesign.fr
flipflopdesign@free.fr

29 // Caroline Faup is FlipFlopDesign, based in Paris. After her artistic studies, Caroline started working as an author and illustrator of children's books and magazines, and as a creative director for a French company specializing in toys, handicrafts and DIY products for children. Immersed in this pleasant universe of drawing, sewing, knitting and customizing, she was able to improve her various skills. Caroline then created FlipFlopDesign, and is now a graphic designer, illustrator and consultant, creating ranges for stationery, decoration, fashion and toys. Caroline loves to create soft colours, vintage patterns and happy animals, and likes to give a positive eco-friendly message about taking care of our environment.

Top / Folies
Printed by Les Contemplatives, these sticker patterns were created for use on the dishwasher, with the idea of decorating a technical object with glamour and retro style.

Bottom / FlipFlopDesign
Caroline's blog header displays the spirit of her style.

Opposite top / Ride Cool
The iconic Eiffel tower is dressed with lace edging in this fun children's poster. Scribbled-effect clouds and trees give it vibrancy. The more you look, the more intricate little details you spot.

Opposite bottom / Grow Trees
This incredibly detailed illustration was created for a children's poster about the environment. Whimsical animals and birds are scattered around a central tree, with layers of texture created from dots, cross-hatch, scribble, and lace.

Overleaf / Happy Folk
Green & Red
These wall stickers, published by Les Contemplatives, have a paisley design and a folkloric spirit.

happy folk

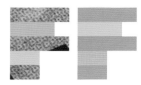

freckleface

www.freckleface.co.uk
tania@freckleface.co.uk

30 //   Based in Nottingham, freckleface is a small greetings card publisher. The founder, Tania Lambert, studied Textiles at Loughborough College of Art and Design, and currently designs work for use on greetings cards and textiles, choosing interesting freelance projects to fit in with her main commitments at freckleface. Tania has always loved collage, seeing it as "like a jigsaw puzzle – you try the pieces together and after a while they all fall into the right place".

Top / Little Fox
Bottom / Dearest Deer
Created from collages of paper and fabric, these designs for cards have an enchanting, storybook feel that would appeal to adults as well as children.

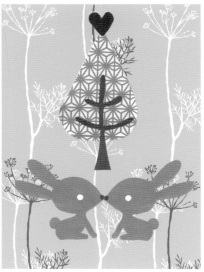

Top left / Mouse with Cakes
Top right / Pretty Kitty
Two more greetings card designs that exude sweetness, with their cute characters and pretty, collaged papers.

Middle & Bottom / Woodland Birdie, Deer, Owl and Rabbit.
Woodland is a range based on the idea of an idyllic British forest, encompassing dappled sunlight and the thrill of spotting an animal for a fleeting instant. Tania found inspiration for the imagery in Scandinavian and folk art of the '60s.

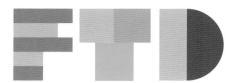

Fred the Dog

www.fredthedog.fr

31 // Fred the Dog was born when Paris-based mother of two Catherine Darmon had an unsuccessful search for fun, original, reasonably priced children's bed linen. Realizing that she might not be alone in her predicament, she decided, after meeting a great textile designer, to create her own line. Since then the bedding ranges have expanded to include cushions, wall stickers, T-shirts and bags. The designs shown here were created by Agnes Larnical.

Right & Opposite
bottom right / Robo
The robot in this design is not aggressive at all, but rather retro and disco, with feet like elephant legs, asymmetric eyes and a calculator on his tummy.

Opposite top &
bottom left / Loco
Evoking illustrations of trains from days gone by, this modern version pays great attention to detail. Each highly stylised carriage is different, perfect for creating stories, and the colours avoid traditional nursery baby blue in favour of a bolder palette.

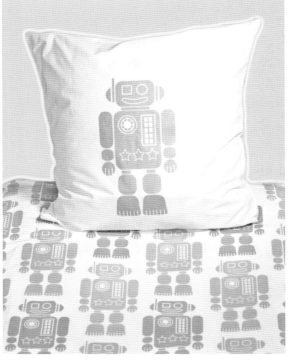

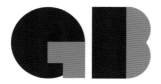

Galia Bernstein

www.nbillustration.co.uk
info@nbillustration.co.uk

32 // Galia Bernstein was born and raised in Israel, and learned Graphic Design while serving in the army and working on their weekly magazine, before becoming the magazine's art director as a civilian at the tender age of twenty-one. She later worked as an art director for children's magazines in Israel, and during that time illustrated around 20 children's books and published kids' comic strips. She moved to New York in 1999 to study at Parsons School of Design, graduating in 2003, and now works as a textile print artist and freelance illustrator. Galia works directly on the computer using Photoshop, and loves using patterns and texture, unexpected colours and limited palettes. Her style is elegant and decorative, and very much influenced by her work as a textile artist.

Above & Opposite / Galia Print
This design was initially created for a promotional canvas tote for Tom Cody Design, a New York-based textile design studio. Galia loves making patterns, and so she turned the original one-colour placement design into a repeating two-colour pattern.

Galison

www.galison.com
sales@galison.com

33 // Galison is a stationery publishing company based in New York. It began life in 1979, working with museums to make their imagery widely available in the form of paper products that were well designed and manufactured. Though this is still part of their core business, they also publish fresh, contemporary designs. Galison's creative director is Juanita Dharmazi, and the team includes editor Julia Hecomovich, and designers Shelby Spears and Sarah Foley. They also have a children's division, called Mudpuppy.

Right / Confetti Garden
A cheerful, collage-inspired design on notecards by Clare Nicolson.

Opposite top & Middle / Retro Tulip
Memo box, sticky notes, and file folder. This '40s- and '50s- inspired floral pattern was based on a design by Lorena Siminovich, but the retro motifs were brought bang up to date with digital graphics, textured ground and a contemporary colour palette.

Opposite bottom left / Scandinavian Modern
This file folder features a crisp, clean, geo-floral design by Salla Kangasniemi from Northern Connection.

Opposite bottom right / Pinwheel
File folder. A set of eight co-ordinating folders where each pattern is based on circles and flowers. The scale and colour of each design is varied, yet they blend perfectly.

RETRO TULIP

sticky notes

480 DECORATED STICKIES IN ASSORTED SIZES

POST MESSAGES AND REMINDERS IN STYLE

RETRO TULIP

file folders

SCANDINAVIAN MODERN

pretty file folders

PINWHEEL FLORAL

file folders

Gemma Correll

www.gemmacorrell.com
gemmacorrell@hotmail.com

34 // Gemma Correll is based in Norwich, where she has lived since studying at the Norwich School of Art and Design, from where she graduated in 2006 with a first-class BA (Hons) degree in graphic design, specializing in illustration. Gemma now works as a freelance illustrator and, as well as undertaking commissions for publishing companies, she also creates her own products that can be bought in various retail outlets, at craft fairs and online. She is also a member of the Fine City Friends, a Norwich-based crafty crew that also includes Kate Seaward, Helen Entwistle and Anthony Zinonos.

Top / Bird Brooches
A sudden nostalgia for childhood crafts inspired Gemma to make these brooches, which comprise simple drawings on shrink plastic.

Middle / Pika Banner
Amy, of Pikaland.com, asked Gemma to create a banner to be displayed at the top of the blog. She chose to create something sweet and quirky, to fit in with the tone of the blog.

Bottom / Sweet Stickers
Stickers are always popular, and fun to buy with pocket money or for a stocking filler. These were mostly inspired by Gemma's obsession with cakes.

Above / Customized Notebook
This notebook was created using a gocco printer for the
basic design, then decorated with marker pens to make
a unique gift.

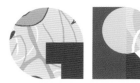

Gemma Robinson

gemmamarierobinson@hotmail.co.uk

35 // Gemma Robinson graduated from the University of Leeds with a first-class BA (Hons) degree in textile and fashion design.
Now based in the north of England, she is currently working to briefs and commissions as a freelance textile and surface pattern designer.

Top / Honeysuckle
A detailed, hand-drawn representation captures the delicate bell-shaped honeysuckle flowers naturally winding around a vine. Layering of foliage adds depth, and the design is finished with ladybirds and sweet pastel shades.

Bottom / Jewels and Beads
A vintage-inspired collection of delicate perfume bottles with free-flowing beads is hand-drawn to depict the intricate jewels, expressing femininity with a contemporary colourful palette.

Top left / Polka-dot Leaves
Simplistic hand-drawn sprigs
with delicate polka-dot
outlines that recreate a soft,
stitched effect are layered with
solid silhouettes that suggest
a natural scattering of leaves.

Top right / Eucalyptus
Branches
Inspired by an initial natural
observational line drawing
and coloured with a refreshing
spring colour palette, this
print subtly combines different
shades and depths of colour.

Bottom / Hummingbird
Inspired to capture the
tranquillity and beauty of
this feeding bird, this design
depicts the precision of
feathers by colourfully layering
different textures and shades
within hand-drawn artwork.

Géraldine Cosneau

www.geraldine-cosneau.blogspot.com
geraldine.cosneau@orange.fr

36 // Géraldine Cosneau grew up and still lives in Nantes, and studied there at the École des Beaux-Arts. She now works as a freelance illustrator on children's books and for kids' fashion ranges.

Top / Christmas Sock
From the series entitled 'Mes jolies cartes à gommettes' published by Lito, this card has a Christmas theme, and was designed to be completed with stickers. The patterned, floral background really makes it stand out from the crowd.

Bottom / Wishes 2008
This was Géraldine's greetings card for New Year 2008, featuring a row of rooftops in a warm colour palette of pink, orange and grey. The criss-cross lines give the otherwise simple forms detail, and the cat gives the design a focal point.

bonne année
2008

Top / Three Little Eggs
Published by Lito, this card, with an Easter theme is part of
a series of four entitled 'Mes jolies cartes à gommettes', and is
designed to be completed with stickers. Three cute characters are
set against a patterned ground, and each egg is also decorated.

Bottom / Peacock
The pictures in this book, entitled *Mes Créations des Quat'saisons:
Le Printemps* and published by Mila, are designed to be completed
with collage, stickers and colouring.

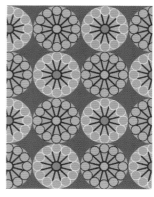

Hang Tight Studio

www.hangtightstudio.com
heather@hangtightstudio.com

37 // Heather Dutton studied for a BFA in fashion design at Savannah College of Art and Design and went on to work as a fashion designer in San Francisco for about seven years. However, she had always been a 'pattern junkie', so she took a leap of faith and decided to start a new career. She moved to an old farmhouse in Kennebunk, Maine, and started her own business, the Hang Tight Studio. Working freelance for a variety of clients Heather has created surface patterns for towels, rugs, dishes, bags, ornaments, wrapping paper, tins, desk accessories and fabric.

Top left / Festibloom
A firework explosion of festive floral blooms rings in the spring/summer season.

Top right / Graphic Pinwheel
Although inspired by the design of pinwheels, the motif has been reinterpreted to create a more graphic pattern.

Middle left / Chickaboom
A playful Easter pattern that would work into spring.

Middle right / Groovy Floral
Heather was feeling groovy the day she created this pattern, and what started out as a digital doodle evolved into a full-blown pattern.

Bottom / Chillout
Heather needed a simple geometric design to complete a collection, so she played around with positive and negative shapes.

Above / Bubble Bears
The bear in this design came
from Heather's sketches.
She scanned them into
Illustrator and used the 'live
trace' feature to maintain the
integrity of the originals.
The rest was just colour
and play.

Happy Kimono

www.happykimono.etsy.com
thehappykimono@gmail.com

38 //   Elle Nelson is the talented designer behind Happy Kimono. Now working as an independent artist in York, Elle has no formal training in arts or graphic design, instead all her skills are entirely self-taught. She has been creating art, making music and taking photographs for as long as she can remember, and now sells her cards, gift tags and notebooks online in her Etsy shop.

Top / Back to Back
Kimono Bunnies
Featuring a mirror image
of Elle's trademark style, this
time set against cool ice blue.

Right / Little Fawns
The bright flowers look vivid
when set against the grey
background, and create
a unique look.

Opposite above /
Kimono Bunnies
Elle creates her designs using
neutral coloured backgrounds
and adding dashes of vibrant
colour. Here they take the
form of flowers within simple
white rabbits, for an image
that is simple but enormously
effective.

Heather Moore

www.skinnylaminx.info
heather@skinnylaminx.com

39 // Heather Moore is an illustrator, designer and writer, living in Cape Town. She has no formal training in illustration or design, and tends to make things up as she goes along, which she says is "quite a good way to learn things fast". Heather freelances as an illustrator, mostly doing work for magazines and advertising, and occasionally exhibits her illustration work in a gallery. In 2007 she started selling her paper-cuts and tea towels online in an Etsy shop, and now has a number of stockists in South Africa, the USA and in the UK. Heather also has plans to put her patterns onto crockery, stationery and even wallpaper one day.

Top / Eep! Slate
The bird pattern is screen-printed onto a cotton hopsack tea towel.

Bottom / Summer Weeds
What started out as a paper-cut of a handful of summer weeds is now a screen-printed design for tea towels.

Top / Eep! Olive
As Heather drew these birds, she thought about the noise they might make, and decided it was 'Eep!'

Bottom / Paper-cuts Studio
Heather made these paper-cuts for fun, turning some small drawings of protea flowers into large paper cutouts. In the end, she used them as the basis of vinyl decals.

Helen Dardik

www.oneluckyhelen.com
Representation: www.lillarogers.com
dardik@sympatico.ca

40 // Helen Dardik is an illustrator, pattern designer, painter and toymaker based in Ottawa. Born in Ukraine, she grew up in Siberia, finished art school in Israel and in 1993 moved to Canada and completed a degree in graphic design. Helen fell in love with illustration and describes her work as a combination of retro whimsy and modern fun.

Top & Opposite / Spring Flowers 1 and 2.
This fun floral design is typical of Helen's vibrant, uninhibited style. A large variety of stylised flowers are set within coloured shapes in either a dark or light base.

Bottom / Lil' Red Ridin' Hood
A pattern using folk fairy-tale motifs and hand-drawn typography. The illustrations are placed within ornate frames.

Top left / Happy Birthday
Top right / Hello
Hand-drawn fonts, characters, and flowers are all brought together with great success in these designs created for a surface pattern and greetings card.

Bottom left / Get Well Soon
Fun lettering in mixed colours adds to the cute design of this card that would surely cheer up anyone who received it.

Bottom right / Button Badges
Designed as a self-promotional tool Helen has decided to use these instead of a business card. Featuring three examples of her work and a specially designed header card.

Opposite / Forest Conversation
Quirky woodland characters are arranged in an interesting horizontal ogee-style repeat, which ties in with the animals' speech bubbles to create a very fluid print.

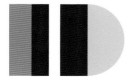

Inkjet Designs

www.inkjet-designs.com
www.inkjet.etsy.com
inkjetdesigns@hotmail.com

41 // Marie Perkins started Inkjet Designs as a side project while working as a textile designer, in order to fulfil her ambition to design for paper goods. She also liked the idea of having an Etsy shop in which to create designs completely to her own brief. The name came from the fact that, in the beginning, Marie intended to print everything at home on her inkjet printer. Marie is inspired by design from Japan and Scandinavia, and a love of graphic shapes and patterns. Recent freelance commissions have included children's placemats, a scrapbook paper collection and greetings cards.

Top / Café au Lait
Inspired by traditional folk designs, and using a decorative, circus-type font, this design was created for coasters and greetings cards. The dark brown background sets off the bright colours which ensure the look remains contemporary.

Bottom / Birdhouse
Created as a greetings card, this modern design uses Inkjet's favoured style of mixing different coloured letters in the text, set on a background of tiny crosses.

Top / Dishwasher Magnets
The Japanese fashion for putting faces onto all manner of inanimate objects provided the inspiration for this design. The fonts also try to express the feeling of clean and dirty.

Middle left / Egg Cups
An Easter card design also inspired by the theme of animating objects by adding faces. Yellow is the traditional colour for Easter and the lace doily provides the perfect device to sit them on.

Middle right / Easter Greeting
Two birds greet each other on this Easter card design. The spring element is added by making the birds' wings from flowers, and the type sits nicely in a cloud.

Bottom / Geo Flowers
Simple circles have been cut and placed to create a pattern.

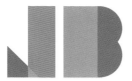

James Brown

www.generalpattern.net
james@generalpattern.net

42 // London-based illustrator James Brown originally trained in printed textiles at Middlesex University. After graduation he worked in the textile and clothing industry, before relaunching himself as an illustrator. Now working freelance, James undertakes commissions for a wide range of clients.

As a reaction to solely designing on a computer, and because he loves the process of print making, James started to produce limited edition screen-prints and linocuts, which are available to purchase through his website.

EXCLUSIVELY FOR OLIVE LOVES ALFIE BY GENERAL PATTERN

EXCLUSIVELY FOR OLIVE LOVES ALFIE BY GENERAL PATTERN

Left / Communication
This motif was designed to
appear on the contact page of
James' website, and is inspired
by Patrick Caulfield and a love
of obsolete technology.

Above / Welcome Dolls
and Welcome Train
These screen-prints were
designed and printed
exclusively for Olive Loves
Alfie, a children's boutique
in Stoke Newington, London.
The idea was to create an
interesting gift choice for
anyone looking to buy for
a newborn. Welcome to
the world!

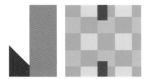

Jannie Ho

www.chickengirldesign.com
jannie@chickengirldesign.com

43 // Born in Hong Kong and raised in Philadelphia, Jannie Ho studied illustration at Parsons School of Design in New York. She worked as a graphic designer for a children's television company, and in publishing as an associate art director, before deciding that illustration was her true calling. Also known as Chicken Girl, Jannie now works in New York as a freelance illustrator for children's books, magazines and advertising, with much of her work and style inspired by Japanese and retro art.

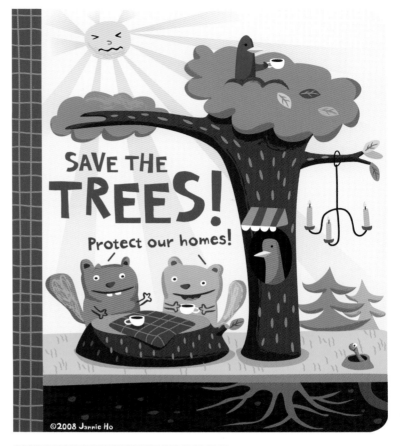

Top / The Wish Tree
This piece, about saving the trees and the earth is especially personal to Jannie and uses playful characters to get the message across.

Bottom / Vroom
Jannie's notepad was used as a promotional item to give out to clients, and is also sold online. Its naive quality is reminiscent of cute Japanese letter sets, and the road design provides the ideal border motif.

CHICKENGIRL DESIGN
Art with Chicken Goodness

The Little Red Riding Hood

©2008 Jannie Ho

Top / Banner
Fun typography perfectly captures the mood of children's book illustration, to promote the Chickengirl Design Blog.

Bottom / Red Riding Hood
Another personal piece, this time exploring textures and lines. The style is fun and friendly with smiles all round, even on the wolf.

Jessica Gonacha

www.jessicaswift.com
jess@jessicaswift.com

44 // Jessica Gonacha is based
in Atlanta and earned a BFA from
Ithaca College, New York. Jessica
now works as a freelancer on a
variety of projects, including
pattern design, illustration and
original paintings for nurseries,
logos, editorial illustrations, custom
wallpaper and fabric. Jessica loves
being commissioned for special
projects and collaborations, and
also sells online in her Etsy shop.

Top / Leaves of Blue
Another pattern inspired by
sketchbook doodles. Jessica
rarely uses deep blues, but in
this instance wanted to try
something different.

Bottom left / Microcosm
Created totally from her
imagination, this pattern
came to be called Microcosm
because it reminded Jessica
of tiny cells, each living their
own tiny life.

Bottom right / Clouds
An uplifting design which
brings clouds to mind.

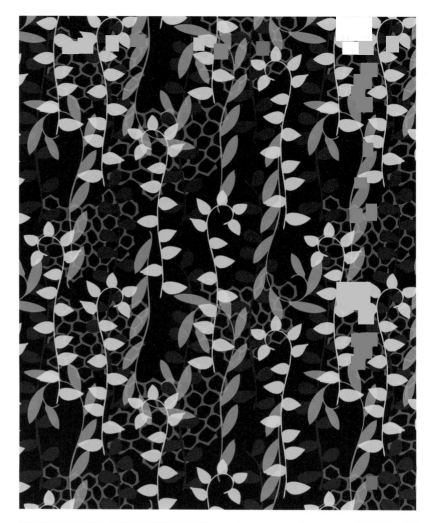

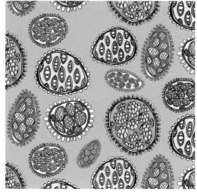

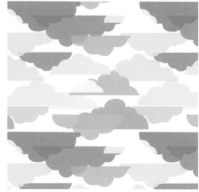

Above / Mimi
Inspired by images in a book of folk-art flowers, Jessica has used solid shapes as coloured shadows behind the shapes in the pattern.

Top / Garden Variety
The flowers for this
pattern came from Jessica's
sketchbook, and she later
added the block-printed
shapes behind them.

Bottom / Blue Spiky Flowers
This design was inspired by
photographs of spiky flowers
in Bertel Bager's book *Nature
as Designer*.

Opposite / Buttercup
This pattern began
life as a single, fun,
flower-shaped doodle.

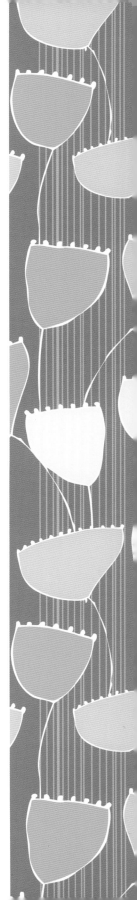

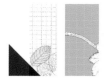

Jill Bliss

www.jillbliss.com
jill@jillbliss.com

45 // Jill Bliss is now based in Portland, Oregon, but her deceptively simple, nature-inspired style stems from her growing up in a do-it-yourself household surrounded by nature in northern California. Combining studio art, graphic design and craft culture, Jill uses everyday items such as pens, fabric scraps, paper cuttings and basic thread to make objects that are unique, including items of stationery, household items, office supplies and artwork. Jill sells her work online or via indie boutiques around the world.

Top & Bottom /
California Rose
This pattern is inspired by the native plants found in woodlands all along the West Coast of the US.

Above / Yerba Mansa
The native herbs that inspired
this print are found all along
the West Coast of the US.

Left / Beach Strawberry
Hand-drawn and digitally
coloured, this print was
inspired by the native plants
found in San Francisco's
Presidio Park and all along
the West Coast of the US.

Jillian Phillips

www.jillyp.co.uk
Representation: www.lillarogers.com
jillygraphics@yahoo.co.uk

46 //   Jillian Phillips studied Fashion Design at Bournemouth and Poole College of Art and Design, before beginning work as a junior graphic designer at a childrenswear forecasting company. Jillian is now based in Brighton and works freelance, doing commissions as requested, and producing work for nationwide clothing and stationery suppliers. Most of her graphics and prints are used on children's clothing and greetings cards, although she has recently started illustrating for children's books.

Top / Owl Aop
Linear flowers beautifully fill the gaps between the owls and birds in this personal piece created in Illustrator.

Bottom / Owl and Tree 2
A brush effect on this tree creates a lively texture on which to sit sweet birds, owls, and leaves made from collaged patterns.

Opposite top / Flowers
Jillian loves using brightened muddy tones on dark grounds, a technique that creates wonderfully bold prints.

Opposite bottom /
Owl and Tree 3
By mixing all-over prints and ditsys, Jillian has created a modern patchwork effect.

Jinjerup

www.jinjerup.com
jinjerup@gmail.com

47 // Jinjerup is designer Chan Lynn, who produces designs for clients from local and international markets. She is inspired by her love for the animal kingdom and the natural sciences. Chan Lynn describes her work as "contemporary, bright, bubbly and loads of fun! Lots of cuteness for babies, children, adults and, of course, animals alike!"

Right / Lekking
Patterns of gathered grouse are laid on a landscape of blossoming vines.

Opposite / Cup-a-cakes
Love transcends all in this scrumptious mix of animals and cupcakes.

Overleaf left /
Treacherous Fruit
Cute fruits are brought to life in the print. The style of illustration is light and fluffy with no hard lines, and an appetizing colour scheme.

Overleaf right / Pitter Patter
A rainbow kaleidoscope of all things natural.

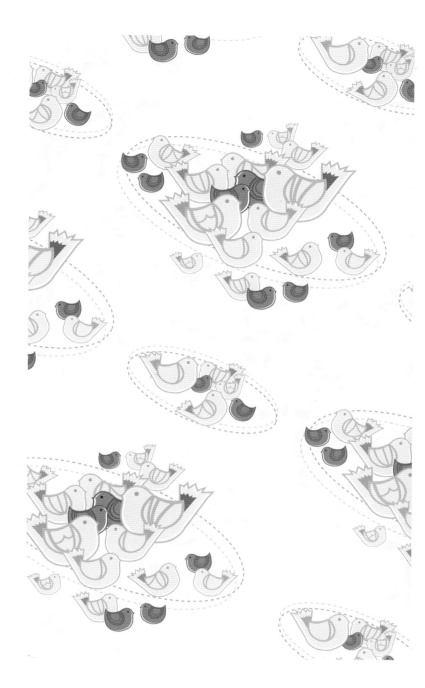

Johnny Yanok

www.johnnyyanok.com
Representation: www.kolea.com
johnyanok@hotmail.com

48 // Johnny Yanok is a freelance illustrator and designer who lives in Akron, Ohio, with his artist wife Jennifer. Johnny is a graduate of Columbus College of Art and Design, and finds inspiration in Mid-century design, vintage kitsch and flea markets. Johnny's unique work merges traditional gouache painting techniques and digital media, and is published by a selection of major stationery brands.

Top / Sewing Basket
Cotton reels and other sewing motifs are brought to life with smiling faces in a design that is built up in layers. The loose threads contrast perfectly with the straight, angular lines of the reels.

Bottom / Meow, Cat Nap, Furball!
Pet designs are always popular and the unusual colours of this print distinguish it from the mainstream. The type gives the layout a grid-like structure.

Opposite top / Dinosaurs
An ideal print motif for boys, and here the dinosaurs have just the right balance between being not too scary but not too cute. The sharp, choppy lines make them appear as if they have been cut with scissors.

Opposite bottom / Sweet Shoppe
In the genre of Japanese Kawaii this fun design features everything sweet. A fluffy effect on the ice creams and cakes provides the movement.

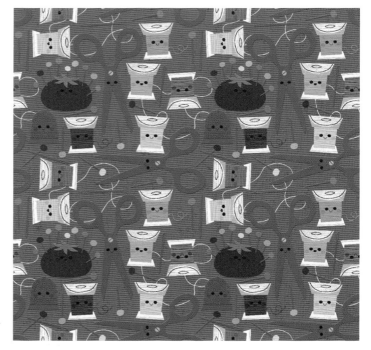

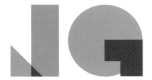

Judit Gueth

www.juditgueth.com
contact@juditgueth.com

49 // Judit Gueth is a Hungarian-born designer and illustrator based in Toronto. Judit studied at the Ontario College of Art and Design in Toronto, and holds an associate diploma in Illustration and a bachelor of design degree. Besides creating illustrations, surface pattern design and graphic design, Judit also applies her designs to stylish home decor items that are socially and environmentally responsible. She introduced her first collection of hand-tufted rugs and wallpaper in 2007, and decorative pillows in 2008. Her rugs are made from 100 per cent New Zealand wool, and the wallpaper is printed on an eco-friendly vinyl-free substrate.

Left / Tomatillo Green
This personal design features a light pattern that has a natural feel to it, and was inspired by the flowers of the Chinese lantern, which turn bright orange in the autumn.

Right / Retro Flowers Pink
Inspired by the floral designs of the '70s, this pattern was originally created for a greetings card line. The simple circular flowers are nicely interspersed with more complicated, spiky ones, providing a good balance.

Julia Rothman

www.juliarothman.com
julia@also-online.com

50 // Julia Rothman is an illustrator and pattern designer located in Brooklyn. Her work can be seen in the pages of *The New York Times* and on stationery and home decor lines. Julia is part of a three-person award-winning design company called ALSO that creates animated websites for small independent companies. For fun, she writes a blog about art and design-related books called Book By Its Cover.

Top / Hello! Lucky Gift Wrap
A collaboration between Julia and the letterpress company Hello! Lucky, these wrapping papers are accompanied by a set of letterpress birthday cards with the same design theme.

Bottom / Tree Pillow
As part of their Artist Series, Urban Outfitters commissioned three pillows focused on a nature theme.

Opposite top / Neighborhood
Commissioned by Urban Outfitters, who gave Julia a vintage swatch of fabric as inspiration, the original brown and pinks palette was changed to a green and blue one and used for a bedspread, notebook and cafe curtain.

Bottom left / Cuckoo Clocks
Each of the clocks was drawn
by hand before being scanned
into the computer to be
coloured and tiled. The design
was sold to Urban Outfitters
and used on notebooks with
a different colour palette.

Bottom right / Wheels
Inspired by '50s flourishes
found in old illustrations,
this was one of the very first
patterns Julia ever made, and
remains one of her favourites.

Kate Seaward

www.ilikepens.co.uk
kateseaward@hotmail.com

51 //   Kate graduated from Nottingham Trent University in 2007 with a degree in Decorative Arts, and now works, under her business name, I Like Pens, as a freelance illustrator. Kate has a number of retail stockists, both online and on the high street, and also sells on her own website. Along with illustration she fills her time with crafty projects to satisfy her love for making, and also takes part in craft fairs.

Top / Busy Bee Notebook
Inspired by her heavy workload and the need for somewhere to make lists, Kate likes the idea of having somewhere nice and humorous to write all the important things down.

Bottom / Tea for Two
This generic greetings card was designed for those times when all you want to say is "Hello".

Opposite / My Best Sketchbook
Kate is inspired by a love for pattern, birds and hand-drawn typography, and works simply with a pen and paper.

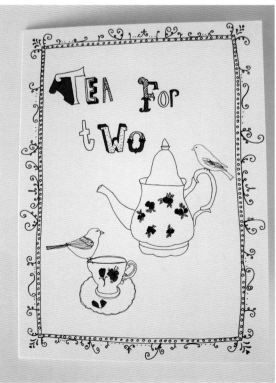

Kate Sutton

www.katesutton.co.uk
contact@katesutton.co.uk

52 //   Kate Sutton has been working as a freelance illustrator for the last few years since graduating from university. Her line drawings and plush creatures are often described as whimsical, and she is influenced heavily by nature, patterns, maps and old children's books. Her work has featured in books and magazines, on buses, t-shirts, plasters, bags and long johns, and she has even done a few tattoo commissions. Kate has taken part in a number of exhibitions as well as producing a variety of limited-edition home-made goodies, such as prints, pirate pigeons and badges.

Top / Brooklyn Flyer
Created for the Renegade Craft Fair in Brooklyn. A loose style of illustration is used in Kate's work which is especially effective on the typography. A simple, muted colour palette makes the buttons really eye-catching.

Middle & Bottom /
Renegade Craft Fair
Various flyers used to promote the fairs, often featuring illustrations of the type of products sold. The eclectic, freehand style adds to the 'hand-made' feel.

Opposite / Tea Habit
Tea and teacups are a recurring theme in Kate's work.

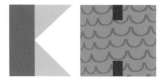

Kathleen Habbley

www.kathleenhabbley.com
info@kathleenhabbley.com

53 // Kathleen Habbley studied literature at college but took up illustration as a hobby after graduation. In 2002 she got involved with the DIY craft movement online and made a website to display her sewn items and illustrations, and things grew organically from there. Her work has been featured in magazines and advertisements and she has also designed company logos.

Kathleen is highly influenced by her childhood: Atari video games; Hello Kitty; Mary Blair storybooks; and Garfield cartoons. She tries to make drawings that would have attracted her attention as a child, and her dream would be to one day write and illustrate a children's book.

ANIMALS

Above / Houses
This is just one of many house drawings Kathleen has made, in a style that is quaint and folksy.

Opposite / Fair
Kathleen was asked to draw a booth at a craft fair, and this is her 'ode to the DIY movement', capturing the colours and creativity of an outdoor market. Kathleen loves adding small details, so that there is a lot to look at when you see one of her drawings.

Left / Animals
In this illustration Kathleen has drawn a self portrait and surrounded herself with animals and pets who provide her with constant inspiration.

Katie Kirk

www.eighthourday.com
www.katiekirk.net
hello@eighthourday.com

54 // Katie Kirk is a graphic designer and illustrator living and working in Minneapolis. With a love of vector art and patterns, Katie is always in the mood to collaborate and create. Together with her husband, Nathan Strandberg, she started EightHourDay, a multi-disciplinary, multi-talented design boutique. Most often found at the studio, the dog park or an antique shop, Katie says "they aspire to the designed life, a place where work, life and inspiration are all equal and integrated organically".

Top / Eli, No! Cover
Inspired by a phrase often said by their nephew, *Eli No!* is a children's book that uses iconic illustrations to tell the story of one trouble-making dog (their own) and the one word that is never far behind.

Bottom / Eli, No! Inside Page
Katie paired bold graphics and bright colours with clean, strong typographic layouts to instantly engage audiences of all ages. A call-and-response writing style makes this book easy to read and even more fun to shout.

Opposite / EightHourDay Pattern
This pattern was created for the 2006/2007 EightHourDay identity and business system, and was used on business cards, postcards, mailing labels, etc. Katie and Nathan liked it because it felt playful and graphic yet abstract.

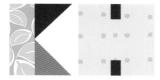

Khristian A Howell

www.khristianahowell.com
www.heathandhowell.com
kah@khristianahowell.com

55 //   Khristian A Howell began her love affair with design in the field of advertising at the University of Georgia, and she discovered the world of textile design while working as a colourist and artist for major US retailer Nordstrom. Today she works as a surface designer and photographer in her own studio, and sells her original designs for apparel, fabric and paper to leading fashion retailers and stationery and wrapping paper companies around the world. Khristian also works on eco-conscious and human-rights art projects with her partner Mary Beth Freet, under the studio name Heath and Howell. Their mission is to use the power of imagery and their love of colour, pattern and illustration to raise awareness of environmental and human-rights issues.

Left / Brellas
Finding a bit of whimsy in the ordinary, Khristian combined hand sketching and digital design for this pattern.

Above / Earth Song
Created by Khristian with Mary Beth Freet for Heath and Howell Art for Humanity, this pattern combines clever illustration with a love of pattern.

Lara Cameron

www.laracameron.com
lara@laracameron.com

56 //   Lara Cameron is a self-taught textile designer from Melbourne. Lara originally worked freelance for a number of years as a web and graphic designer, but eventually shifted her focus to textile design. In 2008 she started up a yardage screen-printing studio called Ink & Spindle with two other creative ladies. Each fabric is printed in Melbourne with environmentally friendly inks onto organic cotton–hemp or cotton–linen blends, and sold online as fabrics or products.

Top / Festive Cooking
Originally designed for the Christmas/seasonal range of online printers MOO, this pattern provides an alternative to traditional religious holiday card designs.

Bottom / My Little World
A regular, geometric repeat is softened for the nursery by the use of decorative edging.

Opposite top / Partridge and Pear Tree
An abstract and modern rendition of the partridge in the pear tree, originally designed for MOO's Christmas/seasonal range.

Opposite bottom left /
Mix Packs
Beautiful, hand-drawn typography and delicious use of colour on header cards really enhance the look of Lara's swatch packs.

Opposite bottom right /
Bulokku Robin's Egg
An abstract, organic print cleverly designed to work as an 'inverse' screen-print. The background colour is printed and the blocks and lines are formed by the negative spaces.

season's greetings

Lark

www.larkmade.com
allison@larkmade.com

57 // In 2005 Allison Jones launched Lark in the UK, and it soon became known for making the sweetest toys and accessories for children. In 2006 Allison moved to rural Australia with her family, but Lark products continue to be sold through UK shops and online, and are also available in Europe, the US, Japan and Australia. Allison continues to make many of the products herself, but also works with local seamstresses. She is also involved with non-profit community groups, including an organization of women artisans in rural Bangladesh.

Top & Bottom / My Best Toy
Lark produces a range of greetings cards beautifully printed with vintage illustrations, such as this calico horse and ride-on dog.

Opposite top /
Vintage Wallpaper
This handmade greetings card uses '60s wallpaper.

Opposite middle /
Wallpaper Card
A classic example of '60s floral design. Allison has been collecting vintage textiles, fabrics, old children's books, retro signs and packaging for many years. She recycles some of these products for Lark to produce hand-made greetings cards.

Opposite bottom left /
Cute Creatures Soap
Lark's cute children's soaps feature a vintage baby animal motif.

Opposite bottom right /
Cute Creatures Badges
This set of three badges features vintage illustrations.

Cute Creatures

Hand made just for you by Lark   www.larkmade.com.au

Lilidoll

http://lilidoll-minidoll.blogspot.com
http://lilidoll.ultra-book.com/
lilidoll_power@yahoo.fr

58 // Lilidoll has been a freelance professional illustrator since 2005, working in France. Lilidoll works mainly in illustration for books, stationery and 'pretty little things', such as pins, pocket mirrors and boxes, although she also makes dolls and soft toys.

Top / Fawn
Little printed missal diary (printed cover and pages) for La Marelle Stationery. This character manages to be cute, and yet at the same time has attitude. She makes great use of traditional patterns, as used here where a lacy heart is set over a harlequin base.

Bottom / Deer Badge
From a set of badges created for La Marelle Stationery. Doe eyes and a quirky outfit give this fawn a unique style.

Opposite / Deer Diary
An ornate, scrolling gold frame gives an air of elegance to this cover design for a diary for La Marelle.

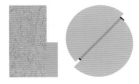

Linda Solovic

www.lindasolovic.com
www.lindasolovic.etsy.com
linda@lindasolovic.com

59 // Linda Solovic runs her own illustration studio, where she works on collages, gifts, stationery and product development and pattern design, and has many well-known clients. Linda also teaches illustration and licensed image design at Washington University in St Louis. Linda finds inspiration in greetings cards, quilts, outsider art, vintage children's illustration of the '50s and '60s, fabric and animated cartoons and films. She is an avid collector of junk and cast-off treasures, found at estate sales and flea markets, which are brought back to life in her artwork. The collages shown here were created to be sold as limited-edition prints in her Etsy shop.

Top / Traci the Bird
For this bird collage, Linda combined her love of '60s pop illustration and one of her favourite colour palettes, pink and orange.

Bottom right / Blooming Buddies Bubble Flowers
This collage series was created on paper that Linda hand-dyed. The quirky and exuberant shapes and colours of the flowers are reminiscent of flower illustrations from the '60s.

Bottom far right / Blooming Buddies Tulips
The limited-edition prints were made using art paper, found paper, ink, pencil and paint.

Above / Julia the Bird
Linda produced a series of bird collages using old book covers
found at an estate sale. Linda likes to name her artwork after
her friends.

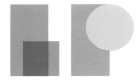

Liz and Pip

www.lizandpip.com
info@lizandpip.com

60 // Liz Smith and Pip Griggs met while working at a design company together. They have been designing under their own label, Liz and Pip, for three years, creating contemporary stationery, wrapping papers and cards. They work in all sorts of hand-drawn media, using Photoshop and Illustrator for scanning images, colouring and designing. Liz trained at the Royal College of Art and lives in London, while Pip trained at Camberwell School of Art and lives in Brighton.

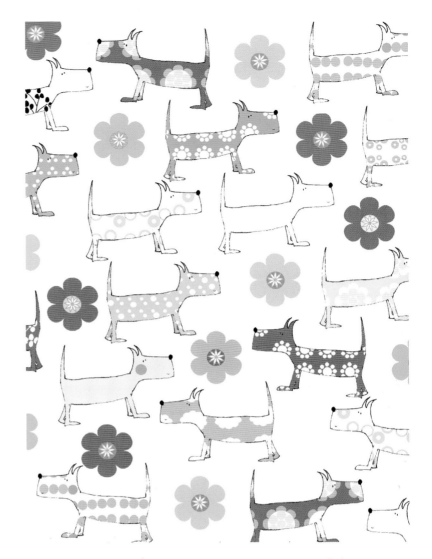

Left / Bird
This notebook cover was
created in Illustrator.

Above / Dog
Created from hand-drawn
images scanned into
Photoshop and Illustrator.
This gives the dog's outline
a pen-and-ink quality.
Decorative patterns are
then contained within
their simple shapes.

Lotta Bruhn

www.bruhnfamily.com
lotta@bruhnfamily.com

61 // Swedish illustrator and designer Lotta Bruhn creates children's books, games and posters, as well as trays, wrapping paper and more from her Malmö-based studio. She is the mother of two girls and two boys. Lotta takes on freelance commissions and sells some of her creations online.

Top / Giraffe Family
Originally created for a children's book this colourful design was later re-drawn to work for a baby's bottle. The animals are reduced to their simplest form and yet are easily recognisable. The thick, white outline makes them stand out from the dark base.

Bottom / Elephant
This tiny elephant repeat was designed for use on a small tray. Everything is kept sharp and simple and varying the colours keeps it from being over busy.

Opposite / The Animals
ABC This print was created as a teaching aid, as well as a decorative nursery item. Lotta has produced both English and Swedish versions. By producing each letter in a different coloured square it not only creates a nice uniform layout, but gives greater scope in playing with the look of the various characters.

Overleaf left / Bullfinches
Designed for Christmas wrapping paper, this pattern has a suitably dark, wintry feel with snowflakes set against a dark sky.

Overleaf right / Pretty
Pretty Elephants
Devised as a fabric print, two mirror-imaged elephants are repeated to create an overall pattern effect.

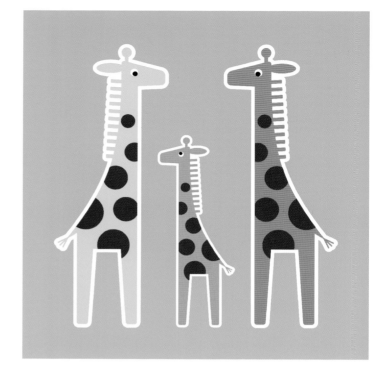

DJURENS ABC

ALLIGATOR · Aa
BÄLTDJUR · Bb
CITRONFJÄRIL · Cc
DROMEDAR · Dd
ELEFANT · Ee

FÅR · Ff
GIRAFF · Gg
HÖNA · Hh
ISBJÖRN · Ii
JORDEKORRE · Jj

KOALA · Kk
LEJON · Ll
MÅNFISK · Mm
NYCKELPIGA · Nn
ORANGUTANG · Oo

PLATTFISK · Pp
QUETZALER · Qq
RÄV · Rr
SKÖLDPADDA · Ss
TVÄTTBJÖRN · Tt

UGGLA · Uu
VAL · Vv
WEDDELLSÄL · Ww
XENOSAUR · Xx
YAK · Yy

ZEBRA · Zz
ÅL · Åå
ÄLG · Ää
ÖRN · Öö

a b c d e f g h i j k l m n o p q r s t u v w x y z å ä ö
A B C D E F G H I J K L M N O P Q R S T U V W X Y Z Å Ä Ö

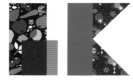

Lotta Kühlhorn

www.lottakuhlhorn.se
lotta@kuhlhorn.se

62 //   Lotta Kühlhorn was born in Stockholm, and studied graphic design and illustration. Since graduating in 1987 she has been freelancing, initially working mainly on book covers, and since early 2000 also with patterns. Lotta's company, Lotta Kühlhorn by Retro.etc, which she started with a friend, produces and sells various homeware items, including trays, cutting boards and mugs. Lotta is a member of The Stockholm Typographic Guild and The Swedish Association of Illustrators and Graphic Designers, and has many national and international clients.

Top / 88 Green
Lotta had the idea to create patterns from numbers and plans to do designs using 1-9. Shown here is number 8. Using the form of the number as a starting point they are modelled into retro-style ogee shapes.

Bottom / Design 2
Made for the Stockholm exhibition of 2002.

Opposite / Mixed Garden
A sketch of vegetables waiting to be developed further. The dark brown base and warm hues of the vegetables create a vivid design.

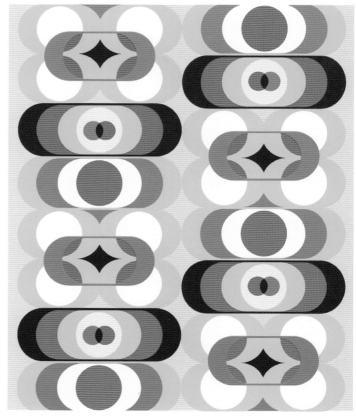

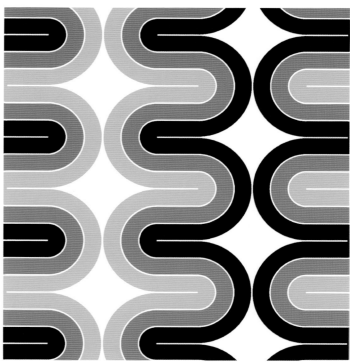

Top / Pears with Red Leaves
Lotta is very interested in
gardening and it shows in
her love of drawing fruit and
veg. The hot colours make
a break from the usual and
the uniform rows of leaves
give it a structure.

Bottom / Seville Orange
Designed for Swedish wine
and spirit shop Systembolaget
for use on their Christmas
packaging.

Opposite / Baby Radishes
A sketch from a series of
root vegetables created for
a decoration in the subway,
Stockholm. The organic forms
of the radishes are pared
down to the point where they
become just shapes.

Lov Li

www.lovlidesign.com
info@lovlidesign.com

63 // Lov Li is a design studio based in Birmingham, established by talented designers Beth White and Rachel Taylor. Rachel studied Textile Design at West Surrey College of Art and Design and has over ten years' experience working as a freelance textile and giftware designer. Beth studied Textiles at Duncan of Jordanstone College of Art and Design and has worked in the fashion industry for ten years. As well as designing their own works, Beth and Rachel represent a select group of creative designers under the Lov Li banner. The result is a very special, highly diverse and exciting collection, available online in their extensive portfolio, for sale and license.

Top / Hello Bunny
A hand-collaged crazy paper design for kids.

Bottom / Hello Bam Bam
A hand-collaged crazy paper design for kids.

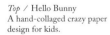

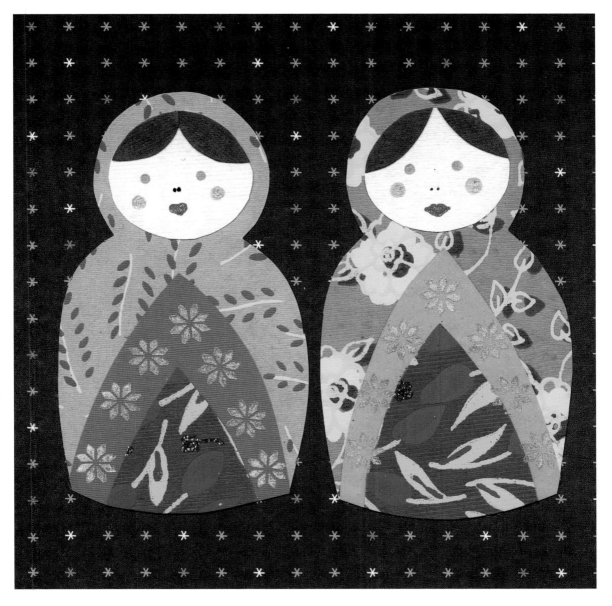

Above / Best Buddies
A greetings card design
featuring two sweet twin
babushka dolls.

Above / Night Owls
A collaged paper design for kids featuring cute owls.

Opposite top left and Opposite top right, Middle left and Middle right / Spike, Ollie and Junior, Robbie and Spot
A whimsical series of cute animal characters designed to give the feel of fabric collages. From their everyday card range.

Opposite bottom left / Kioko
This hand-collaged paper design is from the everyday card range. Kioko is one of Lov Li's most popular designs, and she also features on wall-art prints by US company Oopsy Daisy.

Opposite bottom right / Chu
Chu is a super-cute little Eskimo character, and part of a range of Christmas cards made from hand-collaged paper.

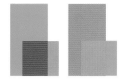

Lovelylovely

www.lovelylovely.co.uk
info@lovelylovely.net

64 // Lovelylovely is the work of fashion designer Louise Scott-Smith and graphic designer Georgia Vaux. Louise is a fashion/textile graduate of Central Saint Martins, and has designed for Emilio Pucci as well as working as a freelance fashion textile designer with clients such as Calvin Klein and Donna Karan. Georgia Vaux studied at Chelsea School of Art and has worked extensively within the world of design. Her recent projects include designing for Japanese fashion designer Yuko Yoshitake. They share an aesthetic vision that has drawn inspiration from diverse sources such as Japanese graphics, Hungarian handicrafts and the books of Marguerite Patten.

Above & Opposite / New York, Paris, Las Vegas, Tokyo and London
The jet-set tea towels – hand-printed in the UK – are inspired by their designers' love of holiday souvenirs, and are an ongoing design project that will eventually include all the big cities of the world.

Lucy Joy Oldfield

www.lucyjoyoldfield.com
lucyjoyoldfield@hotmail.co.uk

65 // Illustrator Lucy Joy Oldfield lives on a wide-beam canal boat in the city of Bath, making friends with the ducks and constantly moving around. She studied for a BA in illustration at the Arts Institute at Bournemouth, and loved being by the sea. Since graduating she has undertaken a wide range of commissions for nationally known clients. Creating patterns is a new-found love and she hopes to find lots more freelance work in this arena.

Above / Chairs
Lucy was inspired to produce this piece by vintage chairs and fabrics for upholstery.

Opposite / High Tea
Commissioned by My Design Company, this illustration was created for a perfume packaging pitch. Using traditional British motifs such as tea cups and roses creates a delicate and feminine design. Muted colours add to the antique feel.

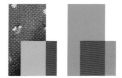

Lynda Lye

www.forestprints.com
info@forestprints.com

66 // Lynda Lye is from Singapore, which is also where she is currently based. She took a bachelor's degree in Fine Arts from the School of the Art Institute of Chicago, majoring in Visual Communications, but for the past four years her full-time job has been concentrating on her lifestyle accessories label, littleoddforest, where she designs and sews cute handmade products. Lynda sells online from her own website and on collective sites such as Etsy, although most of her business is wholesale.

Top / Wee Treeling
After the success of her Treeling plush, which was published in two craft books, Lynda decided to bring newer versions of her Treelings to life, and making a tiny version of the Treeling came very naturally.

Bottom / Mogu
With her first attempt at sewing felt pin brooches, Lynda found the mushroom shape was easy to cut fairly quickly freehand. It was her first submission ever to Fred Flare's Next Big Thing, and it got her in as one of the winners.

Top / Grumpy Raincloud
A collaboration with Claire
Mullan of Tee and Toast, who
proposed that littleoddforest
bring her cute graphic
illustrations to life by turning
them into usable items such
as purses, badges and coasters.

Bottom left / Love Owl
Who doesn't love owls? Lynda
felt she had to make an owl
something, and she couldn't
escape her love of hearts either.

Bottom right / Hoot the
Magnificent Love Owl
This graphic illustration
was originally designed as
a tank-top print, but was
eventually used on a notecard
because it was a little too
'rigid' for a tank top.

Macrina Busato

macrinabusato-design.com
tavitadesign@gmail.com

67 //   Macrina Busato, based in Madrid, became a freelance designer after becoming a mother, and now sells her designs all around the world. She creates patterns for textiles, stationery, paper, wallpaper, packaging and children's products. In 2008 Macrina was the winner of the first European pattern contest Textura Pattern. She also teaches Surface Design at degree level.

Right / Wood
The secret life in the woods inspired this series. Little birds and big oak trunks show a geometrical and linear approach to nature.

Opposite / Easter
This pattern is inspired by the millefiori technique used in Venice for decorating glass beads and vases.

Mademoiselle Dimanche

www.mademoiselledimanche.com
contact@mademoiselledimanche.com

67 // Mathilde Alexandre, a textile designer from Paris, created the brand **Mademoiselle Dimanche**, where she creates designs and textile patterns that she hand-prints onto fabrics using hand-made stamps. She then makes them into cushions, lampshades and other decorative objects, which she sells on her website – where she also sells fabric by the metre. Mathilde also works as a freelancer, drawing patterns and motifs for printed fabrics or embroidery, for various clients.

Top / In the Forest Stamp
Hand-cut stamps are used to print all of Mathilde's fabrics.

Middle / In the
Forest Pattern 2
An all-over motif that almost loses the viewer in foliage.

Bottom / In the Forest Bird,
In the Forest Squirrel
Mathilde's has hand-printed her designs onto fabrics and made them into cushions.

Top left / In the Forest Bird
Top right / In the Forest Squirrel
Part of the Mademoiselle
Dimanche collection where
woodland creatures are designed
using stylised vegetation. The
foliage is carefully manipulated
to give the animals shape.

Bottom / In the Forest Pattern 1
A pattern inspired by traditional
motifs and eighteenth-century,
French classical patterns.

Magnolia Moonlight

www.magnoliamoonlight.com
info@magnoliamoonlight.com

69 // Based in Charlottesville, Virginia, Christina Flowers is an award-winning graphic designer who created Magnolia Moonlight in 2007. Trained as an architect and industrial designer, she approaches her work from many directions. A passion for making, a natural penchant for colour and a love of all things design, are just a few of the ingredients that inspired her to start Magnolia Moonlight. Christina's cards and calendars can be bought online, and she also takes on commissioned graphic design work.

Top / Shout Cards
A six-pack of cards features one for almost every occasion, and because they are bright and cheerful, the message just jumps off the page.

Bottom / Red Bird Blue Bird
These little birds have found their way into many of the Magnolia Moonlight designs, hidden here or there, but Christina decided to make them the stars for these buttons.

Opposite / Shout Calendar
Embracing luscious colours that reflect each season, this playful, fun calender is designed to raise a smile when adding important dates or little reminders to your agenda. Fill in your own speech bubbles to make each day an expression.

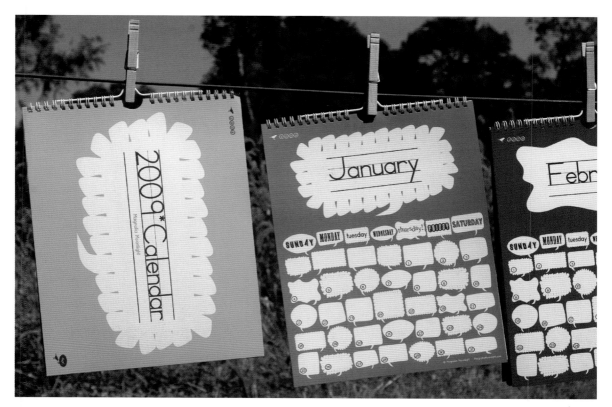

Marie Bushbaum

www.behance.net/mariebee
www.coroflot.com/mariebee
marieb50456@gmail.com

70 // Marie Bushbaum lives and works in Minneapolis. She graduated from Iowa State University and is currently taking night classes at MCAD (Minneapolis College of Art and Design) in screen-printing, letterpress, print and pattern-making, sustainable design and illustration. Marie works full-time as an interactive designer, which means she not only designs websites and web goodies, but anything interactive, including environmental products, print and apparel, in fact anything that enhances the audience's experience. Marie hopes to start her own design studio one day, where she can create fully branded identities.

Top / Final Easter
Coordinates
Half of an egg becomes
a really interesting geometric
in this bold print.

Bottom / Breezy Marine
The horizontal lines on this
scalloped design give it a
highly contemporary look.

Opposite / Final Easter Toss
Cute bunnies, carrots, chicks,
and eggs are scattered or
'tossed' over a textured green
base that evokes the fresh
mood of spring.

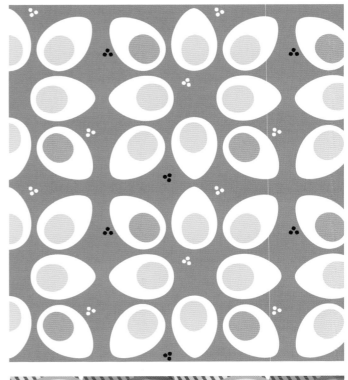

Above / Anthro Floral Main
A loose summer floral pattern
forms the main part of
a fabric collection.

Above / Anthro Floral
For the first co-ordinate the
yellow has been picked out
from the main design and just
the flower centres are used.

Above / Anthro Floral
The second co-ordinate
features just the leaves from
the main print and they are
arranged in a diagonal,
trailing repeat.

Marilyn Patrizio

www.mpatrizio.com
www.sosofties.com
marilynpatrizio@yahoo.com

71 // Brooklyn-based Marilyn Patrizio studied illustration at the School of Visual Arts in New York. She now works as a freelance digital illustrator, but also produces oil paintings and plush toys – otherwise known as softies – which she sells online at her So Softies website and on Etsy, as well as cards, notebooks and T-shirts.

Top / I'm Lovely Pear
This illustration was created for Pear Appreciation Day, a fictitious holiday that Marilyn created on her blog.

Middle / Tea Time
Marilyn's Fuzzy Bunny character enjoys a nice cup of tea on the cover of this limited-edition notepad.

Bottom / Apples
Marilyn is a fan of vintage apple motifs, and created this original apple pattern for her own stationery line.

Opposite / Birds and Mushrooms
This pattern was created for a notecard set, and cleverly uses the round shape of the bird to echo the shape of the mushroom.

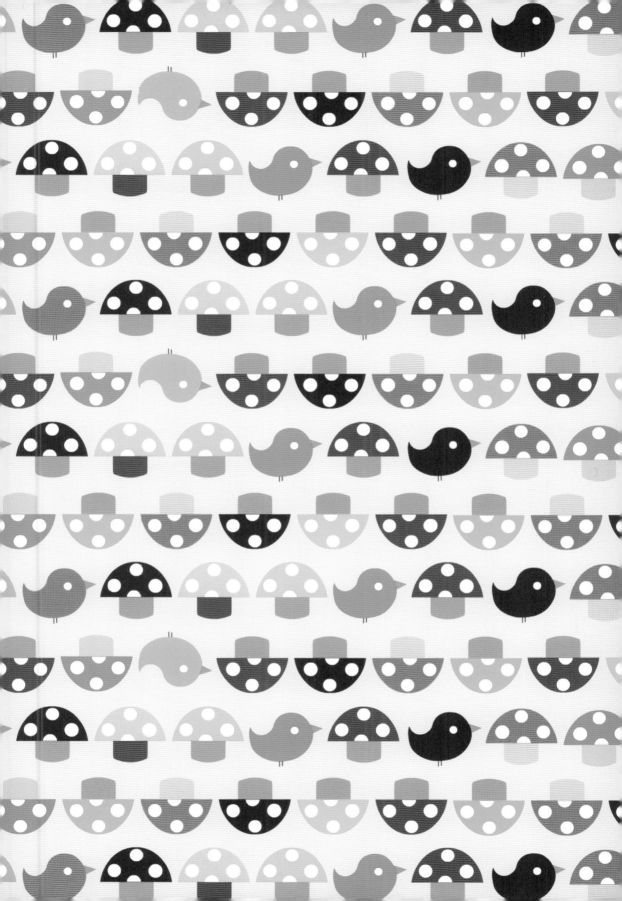

M. PATRIZIO

Opposite / Parachuting Owl
Used on a line of T-shirts, this motif was created to be
a really girly-girl design.

Above / Happy Ice Cream
Created for the cover of a spiral-bound notebook, this illustration
is an ode to Marilyn's favourite type of ice cream: soft serve
in a wafer cone.

Marion Billet

www.marionbillet.com
marionbillet@free.fr

72 // Marion Billet studied children's book illustration for four years at the École Emile Cohl in Lyon. As soon as she graduated, in 2004, she moved to Paris to start her career. Marion now works as a freelance illustrator and has produced work for children's books, advertising, stationery and designs for babies' furniture and clothing.

Above / Animalphabet
Postcard for Cartes d'Art. Delicious French script is used over graph paper to give a schoolbook style to this design.

Opposite left / Cerf
Poster for l'Affiche Moderne. A little deer has antlers draped with interesting objects in this detailed illustration.

Opposite right / Immeuble
Poster for l'Affiche Moderne. Marion's attention to detail is what makes her work so appealing to children. Each floor of this house is filled with action and interest, so there is always something new to see.

Opposite bottom / Carnet Pois
Notebook for Cartes d'Art. A host of different patterns and colours can work together when they are contained in a regulated layout like this one.

Mel Smith

www.melsmithdesigns.com
mel_j_smith84@yahoo.co.uk

73 // Mel Smith obtained a degree in Design for Interior Textiles at the University of Wolverhampton, and is now based in Hampton, Middlesex, where she creates surface pattern designs for her own collection. While at university Mel was chosen in a competition to have her rug and runner designs sold in John Lewis, and she now sells her own wallpapers, notebooks, diaries, magnets, buttons, cards and more online.

Top / Trailing 2
The hand-drawn elements of this pattern – bare winter trees, birds and snowflakes – were scanned to Photoshop.

Bottom / Woodland
This pattern features cute little woodland scenes, Scandinavian style.

Opposite top left /
Henna Circles
For this pattern, which was hand-drawn then scanned to Photoshop, Mel incorporated henna designs into circles.

Opposite top right /
Tree Circles
A winter tree, twisted to a circle motif and repeated, forms a simple but effective design.

Opposite bottom left / Hilly
This fun design was initially inspired by a random '70s motif that Mel found.

Opposite bottom right /
Kaleidospot
For this pattern, Mel layered flower motifs made up of garden tools, such as hand trowels and forks, and experimented with transparency.

Melvyn Evans

www.melvynevans.com
info@melvyn.com

74 // Melvyn Evans has a BA in illustration from Exeter College of Art, and lives and works in Sevenoaks, Kent. In 1992 he was commissioned by a publisher to create the cover artwork for a book, and so began a successful foray into publishing. His work has also been used in design and advertising, and his commissioned and personal work is held in private collections and galleries.

Melvyn draws his inspiration from nature and likes the use of soft, rounded shapes, natural colours and fluid lines.

Above / Bird Pattern
Originally Melvyn's working style was lino print, until he came to use a Mac in 2000. The tails on these birds provide the perfect vehicle to experiment with fancy flourishes.

Opposite top / The Beach
Melvyn uses broad areas of colour accented by line, and likes to spill the colour out of the shapes like a misregistered print.

Opposite bottom /
The Cat is Back
Melvyn's digital work is still influenced by the lino process. Highly stylised trees form the basis of this work, where details like the silver birch bark show real originality.

Michelle Romo

www.crowdedteeth.com
michelle@crowdedteeth.com

75 //   Based in Los Angeles, designer Michelle Romo is entirely self-taught, and started learning how to illustrate and use the computer at the age of sixteen. She now runs her own business, Crowded Teeth, where she designs clothing, jewellery and homewares. In 2007, during her 25th year, Michelle started the 25 Project, and produced an illustration a day for one year, the results of which were turned into an art show and book.

   Michelle describes her style as "cute and Japanese with a Mid-century Modern twist".

Top / Alphabet Kids
Originally created to be used as a font, and later made into a set of flash cards for children learning the alphabet, each of the pictured children has a graphic on their shirt that corresponds with the letter they are holding.

Bottom / Wall Paper
This was the July theme for the '25 Project'. It was drawn over 31 days with little bit being added to the drawing daily. The vertical repeat is anchored around a central house surrounded by all kinds of bizarre motifs.

Opposite / Characters
This was the body of work produced for the December theme for the '25 Project'. The characters range from the cute to the quirky.

Above / Signs and Symbols
This was the April theme for the '25 Project' and features all 30 days of illustration. Taking a look at all the signs she saw around her on a daily basis Michelle decided to re-work them in her own style. It proved to be a great exercise in typography.

Top left / Cutie Trees
The cutie trees are supposed to be made out of candy. This was drawn with the intent of the artwork being printed as fabric.

Top right / Neighborhood
A page from a style guide created for Crowded Teeth for 2008, the neighbourhood is where all of the people of the Crowded Teeth world live, with the exception of Pablo the giraffe.

Bottom left / Woodsy
In another page from a style guide created for Crowded Teeth for 2008, we can see where all of the sweet, fuzzy woodland creatures of the Crowded Teeth world live.

Bottom right / Bird Cages
This pattern was drawn while in an airport as Michelle tried to keep up with the '25 project'. The pattern has a modern folk style using a mirrored repeat.

Mike Lowery

www.argyleacademy.com
Representation: www.lillarogers.com
mike@argyleacademy.com

76 // Mike Lowery likes to draw birds, rabbits and vampire cats. Sometimes they have sweatbands. His work has appeared in galleries and publications worldwide and he is currently working on his first book. Mike lives in Atlanta, where he is Professor of Illustration at the Savannah College of Art and Design. Mike always keeps a sketchbook with him, and is constantly drawing.

Top / Animals and Alphabet
Feeling inspired after becoming a father Mike turned his hand to this delightful nursery pattern. A roughened effect adds a sense of texture to the otherwise flat graphics.

Bottom / Animal Doodles
Created using pencil, silkscreen and digital. This pattern, like most of Mike's, came from scanning in drawings. The hand-drawn black lines give the design a cartoon quality.

Opposite / Nesting Dolls
Pencil, silkscreen and digital. Mike picked up a gocco machine in Japan a few years ago, which allowed him to work at home on silkscreen textures quickly and cleanly. Playing with scale and colour created this interesting layout.

Monaluna

www.monalunadesign.com
jennifer@monalunadesign.com

77 // Jennifer Moore lives in Oakland, California, where she owns her own design studio called Monaluna, specializing in textile and surface design. After studying Anthropology and Design at the University of Minnesota, Jennifer went on to work within various aspects of design, including toy design, surface design and decorative accessories design. She started Monaluna (in its current form) in 2005, originally working as a freelancer, but now focusing mainly on licensing prints, illustrations and artwork.

Jennifer's work allows her to combine her love of painting and all things creative with an interest in people and culture. She loves the energy of the design world, and all the great blogs that keep people connected and excited about design.

Top / Floral
These prints were inspired by big bunches of flowers from Jennifer's local farmer's market. They were painted, originally quite large, using gouache on paper, then scanned in and resized. A license to print the designs onto fabric is held by Robert Kaufman Fabrics.

Bottom / Zen
A pattern inspired by Jennifer's recent trip to Thailand, where flowers and pods are used in everyday decoration and for offerings.

Above / Birds
This print began as gouache on paper, and was inspired by
Jennifer's neighbourhood birds. Jennifer is always amused
and inspired by their characters and physical attitudes.

MOZI

www.mozionline.co.uk
www.mozi.com.au
info@mozi.com.au

78 //   Based in Melbourne, MOZI was founded five years ago by sisters Camilla d'Antoine and Olivia Tipler, and has become renowned for its bold use of colour and lively designs. Camilla studied Fine Art Ceramics and has an honours degree in Visual Communication, while Olivia has a Business/Italian degree. MOZI now supplies over 400 retailers in Australia, New Zealand, Asia, UK and the US, and has its own online store.

   Although her work ends up being produced in many different mediums, from screen-prints to ceramic decals, Camilla always starts with pen and paper, and always includes plants and animals.

Top / Red Wren
Middle / Hummingbird Mug
Mozi designed these hand-decaled bone china mugs with co-ordinating packaging. Silhouettes in a mixed colour palette are arranged over either pale dots or stripes.

Bottom left /
Hummingbird
Bottom right /
Midnight Peacocks
Designed as notepads that double as mouse mats with 50 tear-off pages. On the Hummingbird design the print is faint, which allows you to write over the top. On the Peacocks, clever use is made of the window.

Above / Il Gatto
Screen-printed in Melbourne onto 100 per cent linen, this tea towel design uses Mozi's favoured silhouette style with flowers layered over an elegant cat.

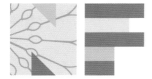

Nadia Flower

www.peepshowsandpuppets.com
Representation: www.illustrationweb.com
nadia@peepshowsandpuppets.com

79 //   "Fragile, delicate, yet graphic and strong," is how Nadia Flower describes the elements that define her illustration work. Combining hand-drawn and computer-based imagery, Nadia works happily across a variety of visual mediums, from fine-art painting to fashion and textiles, as well as pure illustration for the editorial and advertising markets. Based in New Zealand, Nadia has produced work for clients around the world, and her work has also appeared in group exhibitions and book publications in Australia, Japan and the US.

Above / Midnight Express
Part of a collection of fabric and homeware designs, this piece is inspired by Nadia's obsession with headpieces, feathers, costumes and the roaring twenties.

Opposite / Secret Garden
Part of a collection of fabric and homeware designs inspired by the movie *The Secret Garden*. The colour palette and motifs are elegant and highly contemporary with scrolls and feathers adding a real sense of style.

Natalie Tong

www.natalietongdesign.com
www.ahyingmui.etsy.com
natalietongdesign@gmail.com

80 // Natalie Tong was born in Hong Kong, and moved to Vancouver in 1995. In 2006 she attended the Art Institute of Vancouver to study graphic design. Along the way she fell in love with crafting, and hand-sewing felt became her biggest hobby. Natalie has recently graduated and enjoys making craft pieces, which she sells in her Etsy shop, Chi Chi Memories.

Top / Birdie Brooch
Made from felt and fabric, patterned swatches are used on the bird's chest to add character and interest.

Bottom / Owl Sticker
The owl is printed on off-white paper to create a handmade look, and typographic messages have been added to his body. Dashed lines on the border reflect the hand-stitching style of Natalie's products.

Top / Chi Chi Babies
Doodled characters from
Natalie's sketchbooks are
turned into products for
her Etsy shop.

Bottom left / Birdie Sticker
Created for Natalie's Etsy
Shop using textured paper,
the same bird motif from the
felt brooches is used on printed
stickers. Flowers add a
cute touch.

Bottom right / Cupcake
This design is printed on to
textured paper and turned into
stickers using a mini sticker
maker. The cupcakes have
been given all sorts of different
expressions for a fun effect.

Nathalie Lete

www.nathalie-lete.com
nathalie@nathalie-lete.com

81 //   Paris-based artist Nathalie Lete first studied Fashion, and then Lithography, at the Beaux Arts Academy of Paris, and has been working freelance ever since. Her favourite themes are souvenirs of Paris, toys and flowers, insects and birds. Nathalie likes to work with acrylics on paper or cardboard, as well as using her work on mediums such as fabrics, rugs and ceramics. Nathalie runs her own label, Les Editions de Lété, collaborates with other companies and licenses products in Japan under the name Chat Chien.

Top / Eiffel Coeur
Souvenirs of Paris make up a popular theme for Nathalie, and the one people ask for most, especially in Japan.

Bottom left / Ouaf
This design is inspired by Nathalie's collection of toys from her own childhood and those found in flea markets, and has been used on a porcelain box for Asiatides.

Bottom right / Nous Deux
Acrylic on paper.

Opposite / Mon Coeur
Using collage and acrylic on cardboard.

Overleaf left / Textile Print
Originally designed for bed linen, this design was used for
a notebook by La Marelle Editions.

Overleaf right / Poupée Chiffon
When she was young, Nathalie collected fabric dolls and filled
her bed with them.

81 / Nathalie Lété

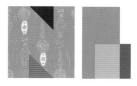

Nicky Linzey

www.nickylinzeydesign.co.uk
www.nickylinzey.blogspot.com
njlinzey@globalnet.co.uk

82 // After studying printed textiles at West Sussex College of Design, Nicky Linzey began hand-painting her patterns onto silk and making cushions for Harrods and Harvey Nichols in London. This developed into other areas of design, and she now works as a freelance designer and illustrator. Nicky is fascinated by colour, texture, shape and pattern, and mostly draws with pen and ink, before colouring digitally.

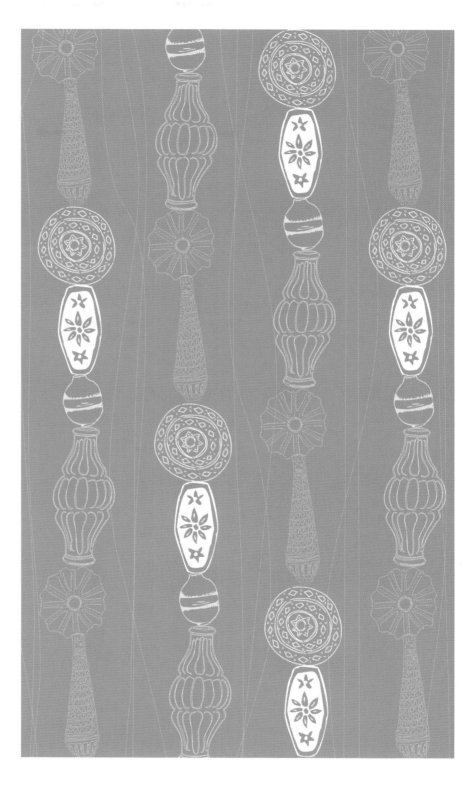

Left / Mosaic Paisley
Nicky loves the work of Antoni Gaudí, and this design, drawn
with pen and ink then digitally coloured, was inspired by the
decorative patterns in his architecture.

Above / Bead Strings
This pen-and-ink illustration was inspired by glass and silver
beads collected over the years from broken necklaces.

Nicola Jane

www.nicolajanesboutique.co.uk
enquiries@nicolajanesboutique.co.uk

83 // Nicola Jane graduated with a BA and an MA from Nottingham Trent University and began working as a designer and agent for a textile studio, with her designs being sold to well-known international textile companies. Nicola designs textiles for childrens-, mens- and womens-wear, using a variety of styles from loose to botanical. She loves to draw and create characters that have featured on a range of cards and stationery. Alongside this Nicola has a small range of accessories including badges and compact mirrors that have been sold in various retail outlets.

Right / Numbers
Nicola has always loved text and numbers and wanted to produce a piece that celebrated the process of 'working things out' and the beauty of mistakes.

Opposite / Tree and Man
Nicola loves sketching, and this piece is a repeat of a view from outside her old studio in south London.

Olive and Moss

www.oliveandmoss.com
info@oliveandmoss.com

84 // Nina Clarke, founder
of Olive and Moss, studied at
the Wimbledon School of Art
and Edinburgh College of Art,
specializing in printed textiles.
After graduating she worked as a
print designer on freelance projects
for popular clothing ranges, and
spent three years at Monsoon/
Accessorize, where she learned to
turn her hand to the many design
demands that came her way.
Setting up Olive and Moss came
from a desire to work for herself,
coupled with an identification of the
limited babywear that the high street
had to offer. Nina's designs are based
around her little animal characters,
each with their own name and identity.
Today the range continues to grow,
with 60 pieces in the collection, as
well as stocking over 150 boutiques
in the UK and several overseas.

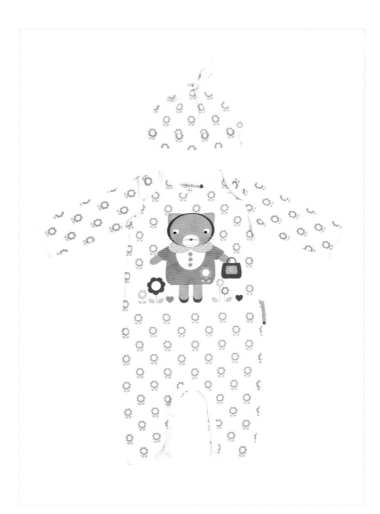

Top / Catriona the Cat
This cat is a new character
who likes her shopping,
and is featured with shopping
bags and accessories.

Bottom / Douglas the Dog
With his neckerchief and
kennel and bone, Douglas is
a special dog with a big heart.

Top / Characters
Olive and Moss characters include Perry the Panda, who has been a bestseller since day one, Louis the Lion, Betty the Bunny and Otto, the big-eyed wise owl.

Above / Margot and Mo the Mice
These mice make a pretty, girly option, and customers seem to love the details in their clothing and printed dresses.

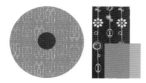

Olli & Lime

www.olliandlime.com
karen@olliandlime.com

85 // Karen Ronneback is a designer of contemporary children's furnishings with as much emphasis on the parents' taste as that of the children. Her business, Olli & Lime, was borne out of a realization that the majority of children's furnishings conformed to a very obvious stereotype. Her idea was to design original creations that stood out in the marketplace and offered a real choice for parents. Designs span co-ordinated bedding, wallpaper, pillows and prints.

Karen also runs a graphic design studio alongside Olli & Lime, designing for print and web.

Top / George Wallpaper
A pattern that would equally appeal to boys or girls, and provides the perfect backdrop for any child's bedroom.

Bottom / Carrie Wallpaper
This contemporary pattern is designed to be adored by girls, but without conforming to the pink fluffy stereotype. The sage-coloured shoe-print wallpaper is printed on heavy-weight FSC-certified paper.

Top / George Bedding
Creating stylish and contemporary bedding with striking use of colour on a contrasting white background was the thinking behind the George bedding range. The lime and milk chocolate design is printed using low-impact, water-based inks on 100 per cent organic cotton percale.

Bottom / Oliver
The aim of the Oliver range was to create a unique, sports-themed print that would appeal to boys, yet retain the contemporary Olli & Lime style.

Orla Kiely

www.orlakiely.com
online@orlakiely.com

86 // Orla Kiely graduated from The National College of Art and Design, Dublin, and continued her education with a masters degree taken at the Royal College of Art in London. She launched her own business in the '90s, and brought a freshness to the fashion world with her use of colour and graphic pattern. Orla's classic signature stem print has become a highly recognizable international brand, and besides her womenswear and accessories collection, she has also expanded into homewares. She has a flagship store in London's Covent Garden, and design studios in the city, and her products can now be found all over the world.

Right / Striped Petal Print
Different shades of the same hue are used to create strikingly vivid retro floral design.

Opposite / Apples & Pears
Orla is inspired by the design of the '60s and '70s, and this print shows her love of repetition and organic shape.

Overleaf left / Multi-stem Print
Orla's signature stem print has become instantly identifiable. It perfectly encapsulates her use of colour and form.

Overleaf right /
Flower Blossom Print
Layers of opaque circles are built up to create a vivid flower set on a cross-hatch, textured stem.

Opposite / Flower
Abacus Print
Simplified flower shapes are
set onto a stripe at different
levels to create an almost
abstract design.

Top left / Pear Print
Beautifully shaped pears
interlock in this bold design.

Top right / Tulip Print
A limited number of dark
colours give this design a
sombre simplicity. The layers
of the tulip are built up with
opaque shapes.

Bottom / Car Print
Created for a travel range,
this design finds the simplicity
and order in having one motif
regularly repeated.

Paperchase

www.paperchase.co.uk
write@paperchase.co.uk

87 // Paperchase is renowned for its design-led and innovative stationery. With over 100 stores in the UK, and concessions worldwide in Borders' stores, it is truly the brand leader in its field. With a talent for adding wonderful surface designs to hundreds of products, such as wrapping papers, magnets, stationery, letter sets, notepads, mugs, diaries and so much more, it has won itself a dedicated following of customers. Besides its own exclusive ranges, it also supports independent card publishers, and you can always find the latest greetings card trends in-store.

Right / Lisa Floral
This autumn season design, created by Lisa Gomez and Paperchase, was used on a wide range of products, from wrapping paper to umbrellas. The flowers are ornately decorated with organic lines, some filled with varying shades of colour.

Opposite / Pet Chopz
Created by Adrian Hunter, Ceri Bates, Trond Friestad, Lisa Gomez and Paperchase, this fun design appeals to customers of all ages. A closer inspection reveals the details given to the characters, such as denim, gingham and knit.

PataPri

www.patapri.com
info@patapri.com

88 // Yuko Uemura is originally
from Tokyo, but now lives in Chicago.
She studied graphic design at
Columbia College Chicago, then
worked as a freelance graphic
designer in Tokyo. When she
returned to Chicago in 2005, Yuko
took a screen-printing class and fell
so in love with printing on fabrics
that she has been doing so ever since.

In April 2007 Yuko started
PataPri, where she designs, prints
and sews all her creations. Yuko
mainly makes kitchen towels, but
also produces bedding, pillows and
paper products. Her inspiration
comes from nature, colour and shapes,
and she loves simple, clean design.

Top / Onion
Yuko has used simple lines
to create this onion design.

Middle / Doors
Five colours are used for this
hand screen-printed pattern,
inspired by walking down
the street and noticing all the
different kinds of doors.

Bottom / Apples
Screen-printed by hand on
100 per cent linen, this was
one of Yuko's first designs.
The beauty is in the shape
of the apple and its inspired
colour scheme.

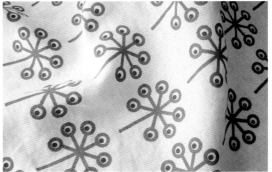

Top left / Trees
Yuko enjoys designing trees, and uses simple shapes with a teardrop inside to represent water.

Top right / Elephant
This dancing elephant is part of an animal collection.

Bottom left / One-year Anniversary Edition
A limited-edition kitchen towel showcases PataPri's designs from the first year of trading.

Bottom right / Dot Trees
For this pattern Yuko has created a line and dot pattern with simple shapes.

Pattern People

www.patternpeople.com
info@patternpeople.com

89 //   Pattern People, based in
Portland, Oregon, was founded in
2007 by designers Claudia Brown
and Jessie Whipple Vickery.
Together they create surface designs
for fashion, paper goods and interiors,
using a variety of media including
paints, inks, graphite and pixels.
They are inspired by everything
from nature to fantasy and fashion,
but always stay committed to their
own vision.

Left / Sky Lights
Designed by Jessie Whipple Vickery for their client Madame of the House, this pattern was inspired by the constellations seen in the night sky.

Above / Floating Flowers
This pattern was created for Tenth and Grant, for use on their environmentally-friendly paper goods. Due to the Japanese-style pattern in the background the flowers really do appear to float on the top.

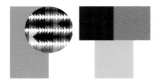

Pavilion Tone

www.paviliontone.blogspot.com
pavilion.tone@googlemail.com

90 // Katie Bean set up Pavilion Tone in the summer of 2008, and now works as a freelance print designer based in southeast London. After graduating in 2007 Katie spent 12 months producing prints and patterns every day, sometimes 20 in one hour, to progress her style. Her work is geometric, with bold, colourful, retro prints inspired by living in London. She has produced designs for major clothing lines and featured in the Future Trends 09 book, in a selection of the most exciting graduates in London.

Opposite / 511
A folksy '70s print that started life as a hand-drawn sketch, then digitalized and coloured in Illustrator. Katie likes to use colours that look slightly aged and yellow.

Above / 412
Katie has overlapped triangles again and again, with the aim of producing the effect of overlapping coloured acetate. The colours were taken from a selection of Polish folk-art paintings she was researching at the time.

Peagreen

www.peagreen.co.uk
www.hellopeagreen.blogspot.com
izzy@peagreen.co.uk

91 // Peagreen have been producing surface pattern and illustration designs for fashion, home furnishings, stationery, interiors and other products for close to 15 years. Starting with just one designer, they now have a multi-disciplined team of nine designers with backgrounds in knitwear, graphic design, illustration, printmaking, textiles and furniture design. The studio is based in the heart of Winchester, Hampshire, from where they have produced work for major clothing and homeware brands. Peagreen also produce their own range of holiday-inspired cards for the Museum of Modern Art in New York each year.

Peagreen thrives on a love of beautiful design, and they always try to produce things that they themselves would love to own or wear.

Top / Special Flo
Designed by Lisa Barnes-Orlandi for Anna Thomas, this folky design has a Scandinavian feel.

Bottom / Torch
Created for Gap Girlswear by Dan Walters, the hand-drawn and vector elements of this design take their inspiration from nature and the great outdoors, as well as urban art.

Opposite / Floral
This modern vector floral by Dan Walters was created with wrapping paper in mind, and although it was produced in Illustrator, it has a feeling of fabric from the '60s.

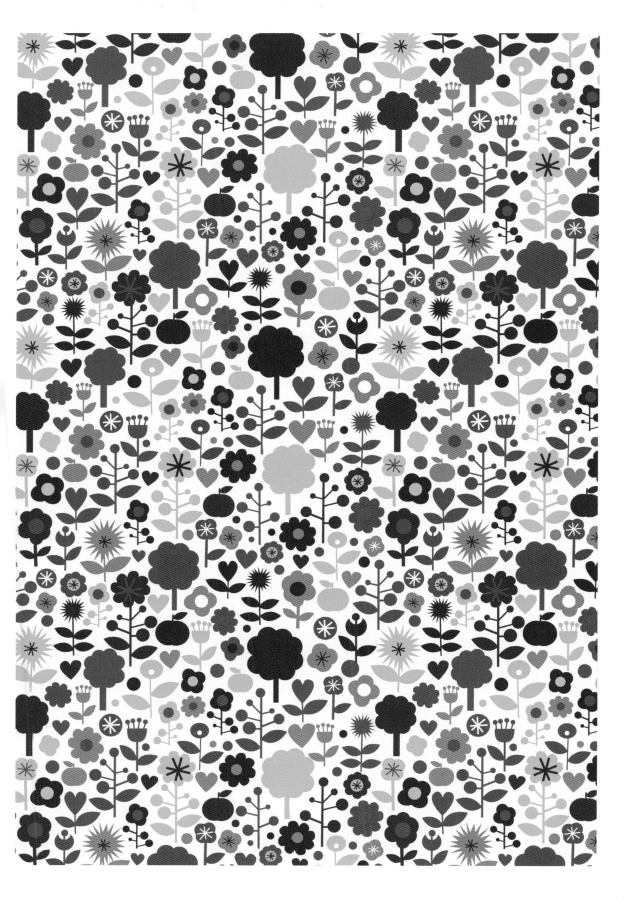

Opposite / Peaspace Print
Created by Dan Walters for the Peagreen website, this design
represents the studio as a whole by using elements of the work
of all of the designers that were there at the time. It has also been
adapted into fluorescent pink and reproduced for their stationery,
business cards and packaging.

Above / Owls
Created by Dan Walters for an apron for Kitsch N Glam,
the design was hand-drawn with thick and thin markers
and finished in Illustrator.

People Will Always Need Plates

www.peoplewillalwaysneedplates.co.uk
info@peoplewillalwaysneedplates.co.uk

92 // People Will Always Need Plates was launched in 2004 by Hannah Dipper and Robin Farquhar. Their aim is to "use high-quality, low-volume batch production to create witty, thoughtful and stylish products as a direct antithesis to the current proliferation of cheap, throw-away design". Hannah is an ex-RCA ceramicist, while Robin studied Industrial Design at Brunel University, and together they offer a complete service for product, graphic, exhibition and interior design.

Top / Trellick
Erno Goldfinger's Brutalist masterpiece has captured the imagination of many a Londoner, and this concrete edifice is celebrated with a limited edition of Trellick Tower dinner plates and mugs. In collaboration with the London Cushion Company, this design now also features on cushions.

Middle / Barbican
The Barbican, in the City of London, is one of the great works of Chamberlin, Powell and Bon. As Robin puts it "We love it, architects love it, many live there, sadly we cannot – for shame."

Bottom / De La Warr
A design commissioned to celebrate the reopening in 2005 of this beautiful '30s seaside pavilion, which is now one of the largest contemporary art galleries in the south of England.

Top / Barbican Tea Towel.

Middle / Greenside
This design was commissioned as a fundraiser for the charitable body The 20th Century Society, to cover the legal costs resulting from their litigation against the owner of Greenside who illegally demolished it, contrary to Grade II listing regulations.

Bottom / De La Warr Mugs

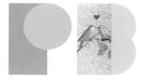

Petra Boase

www.petraboase.com
info@petraboase.com

93 // Petra Boase graduated from Manchester University with a degree in textiles in 1991. Soon after she was to be found presenting on *Change That* for the BBC, rejuvenating tired furniture and household items. She also published many books on crafts and decoration. In 2000 Petra launched her own range of products featuring her now fully honed design style. From a core of collage canvases and handmade greetings cards, the collection has grown to include homewares and babywear, and is available in fashionable boutiques and big-name stores around the world, or from Petra's own online shop.

Top / Lovebirds 3
A design for a greetings card that features two removable button badges.

Bottom / Owl Card
Making designs from vintage scraps is Petra's trademark. This owl has the added benefit of googly eyes.

Top left / Doiley Love
Birds Card
Made from a collage of cut-out vintage pieces and framed by a paper doiley. Also features a removable heart badge.

Top right / Lovebirds
Button badges featuring two birds enhance the appeal of this card design, which also features a decorative font.

Bottom left / Canvases
Petra digitally prints her designs onto high-grade canvas to make an eclectic range of wall art.

Bottom right / Love Bambi Framed
Another example of beautiful vintage collage featuring two doe-eyed bambis.

Above / Pets Wrapping Paper
Charming animals made from
a collage of vintage paper,
fabric, and buttons are
featured on a background
of graph paper.

Opposite top left /
Pink-Framed Love Birds
The subtle, vintage-style birds
are surrounded by a garland
of flowers; a bright pink frame
adds a contemporary touch.

Opposite top right / Tin Cards
Vintage images are enhanced
with tin bird badges to create
a stylish card.

Opposite middle /
Flower Cards
Crafted from vintage wallpaper
and embellished with buttons
at the centre for a retro look
with a modern twist.

Opposite bottom left /
Love Mugs
Petra's collage designs have
been printed onto mugs.

Opposite bottom right /
Notebooks
Vintage-style animals adorn
a set of plain paper notebooks.

Present & Correct

www.presentandcorrect.com
info@presentandcorrect.com

94 // Since 2003 Present & Correct have been cutting and pasting from their front room in London, creating paper goods and selling them far and wide. The founders are graphic designers and illustrators by trade, with a long-term obsession with stationery and paper that has culminated in a constantly evolving online store, which sells Present & Correct's own designs as well as those of other designers from around the world.

Pie & Peas

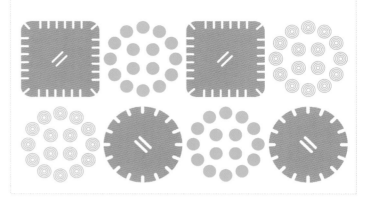

Jelly & Ice Cream

Top / Pie & Peas
Present & Correct have developed patterns using the shapes and colours of some timeless food pairings.

Bottom / Jelly & Ice Cream
The classic British 'caff' is an institution in decline, so Present & Correct wanted to create something that celebrated it and the food it serves.

Opposite top / Bangers & Mash
Letterpress was used to print the cards, giving them extra depth and tactility.

Opposite bottom / Roly-poly & Custard
The designs are elegant and a touch retro.

Bangers & Mash

Roly-poly & Custard

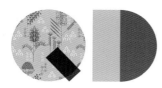

Quyen Do

www.quyen.com.au
quyen@quyen.com.au

95 //   Quyen Do is based in Perth, Western Australia. She designs and hand-prints for her own range of hemp, bamboo and soy fibre handbags, which are stocked around Australia and are available online. Quyen Do also undertakes freelance digital textile design for fashion and homewares clients. Her designs are applied to shoes, stationery, clothing, accessories and more. Qualified in architecture fashion and textiles, Quyen Do uses digital design tools, but always begins with a hand-drawn or painted starting point.

Right / Australiana
The brief for the Botanicals exhibition at Object Gallery in Sydney called for designs inspired by Australia's unique flora, which Quyen has always loved and tried to interpret in a modern way. Quyen chose a geometric approach to the interpretation of the banksia, wattle, bottlebrush and grevillea.

Opposite / Elephant Bird
Hand-drawn and digitally designed, this is the signature print for Quyen's second range of hemp, bamboo and soy fibre handbags. She wanted to create something fun, with a mix of themes, including fruit, animals and floral pattern.

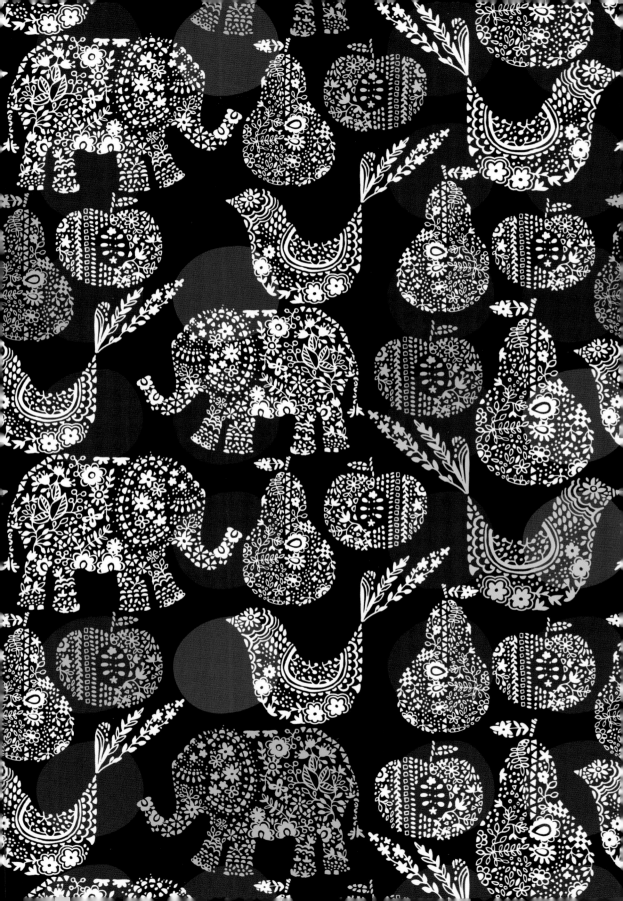

Rachael Taylor

www.rachaeltaylordesigns.co.uk
rachaeltaylor_design@live.com

96 // Rachael Taylor had three years' industry experience before setting up as a freelance surface pattern designer. She now designs for the textile, interior, fashion and greetings industries from her Leeds-based studio. Rachael graduated with a BA (Hons) in textile and fashion design in 2005, and soon after she held her first solo exhibition, 'Stitched', featuring 30 screen-printed textiles. Rachael loves to draw and doodle and add spontaneous energy to her work.

Top / Blue Doodle Flower This design, created for the home page of Rachael's website, reflects her personal style of loose linework, silhouettes and textures.

Bottom & Opposite bottom / Snowflake The snowflake was created for Rachael's personal greetings portfolio, to demonstrate a contemporary Christmas look. Lined paper and hand-drawn motifs have been scanned in and combined with computer-generated motifs.

Opposite top / Blue Doodle Placement Loose, hand-drawn doodles from Rachael's sketchbook are combined with textures to create a layered look.

Rachel Harper

www.rahrahrepeats.blogspot.com
rachelaharper@hotmail.com

97 // Rachel Harper is a full-time freelance designer based in Nottingham, who has been designing for giftware since graduating in 2005 from Loughborough University, with a BA (Hons) in illustration. During this time her designs have been licensed worldwide for the greetings market as well as for scrapbooking, apparel and homeware. Her designs have also appeared in several shops on the British high street, including John Lewis.

Left / Floral Fancy
This ditzy floral print was created in Adobe Illustrator using a limited colour palette, and would work equally as well for fashion as for paper products.

Above / Happy Bird Day
This birthday bird design, created with wrapping paper in mind, combines simple shapes, pattern and typography to create a fun, fresh approach to a birthday celebration.

Rock Scissor Paper

www.rockscissorpaper.com
info@rockscissorpaper.com

98 // Susie and Heidi Bauer are sisters and owners of Rock Scissor Paper. They have been designing and making stationery and gifts since 1993, and today Rock Scissor Paper has a full line of stationery with more than 500 products, including greetings cards, thank-you cards, blank notecards, invitations, gift tags, enclosure cards, journals and an extensive holiday card line. From their Los Angeles base they ship all over the world.

Top / Crafty Mushroom
The vintage fabric pieces make each card unique.

Bottom / Crafty Birds
Over the years the sisters have saved loads of vintage fabric scraps that were just too good to throw away. They felt that they could be used to create something really cute in the future, and they were right, as the cards in this range prove.

Rubbergob

www.rubbergob.com.au
info@rubbergob.com.au

99 // Rachael Barkess and Janine
Finnie are Rubbergob, based in
Perth, Western Australia. The pair
mostly work on retail design and
branding, followed by illustration
and pattern design, but they would
be deliriously happy if this were the
other way round. As well as their
own patterns and surface designs,
Rubbergob also take commissions
from retailers and companies.
They create designs across many
styles and with many mediums in
mind, but all reflect an irreverent
humour and quirky style.

Top / Wooden Owls
Wallpaper owls sit on a branch
below wood-panel skies.

Bottom / Wallpaper Birds
This design is based on a little
Australian bird called the willy
wagtail, which is very small
but brave enough to challenge
the enormous kookaburras.

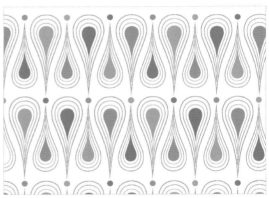

Top left / Green Tree
This environmental image
is used on a notebook, pillow
and organic tote.

Top right / Smile Flower
From the Let's Get Happy
collection, this flower
is designed to add a dose
of 'happy' to your home.

Middle left / Trees Pattern
A colourful and bold pattern
designed to bring elements
of nature into the kitchen.

Middle right / Drops Pattern
This colourful graphic pattern
was used on products such
as coasters and tea towels.
The sisters deliberately chose
a bright, poppy colour scheme.

Bottom / Applestack
From the Let's Get Happy
collection, this cute design
featured on a pillow and tote
bag. Susie and Heidi came up
with six happy slogans, then
developed artworks that fit the
spirit of each of the sayings.
The designers were inspired
by silk-screened artwork
from the late '60s and early
'70s, which often included
hand-drawn lettering that
packed a strong visual punch.

Above / Emma's Owl
This retro-style design has buttons for eyes and a paper collaged body that will appeal to all ages. The whole thing is set off by a harmonious background pattern.

Right / Papertree
A wallpaper tree with patterned leaves sits on an icy blue sky background.

Far right / Numbers
Wallpaper numbers are perfect for the little mathematician.

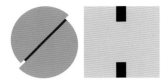

Samantha Hahn

www.samanthahahn.com
www.samanthahahn.com/blog
samanthahahn@gmail.com

100 // Samantha Hahn is an illustrator, surface pattern designer, crafter, blogger and art teacher. She earned a BFA in illustration from Syracuse University and an MA in Art Education from Teachers College, Columbia University. Her studio is in Brooklyn, and her clients include national magazines and greetings card companies. Samantha also sells prints of her work in the online shops Little Paper Planes and Shiny Squirrel, and keeps a design blog called Maquette.

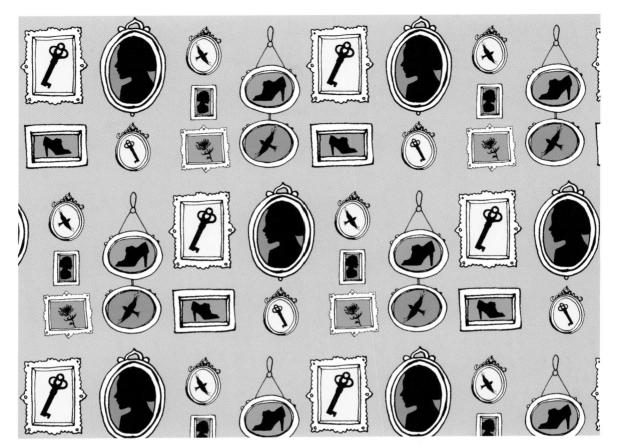

Opposite / Geo Notecard
The geometric shapes are
rendered by hand and
slightly imperfect.

Above / Frames
This pattern is a whimsical
and quirky take on the
traditional framed silhouette.
American Greetings licensed
a variation on the same theme
in a holiday colour scheme.

Left / Elephant Baby
Announcement
Samantha has used a gender-
neutral palette that still
manages to feel soft and
inviting, surrounding the baby
elephant with a regal frame.

Sandra Isaksson

www.isak.co.uk
www.sandraisaksson.com
info@isak.co.uk

101 // Sandra Isaksson is a Swedish graphic designer and illustrator who divides her time between freelancing for other companies and designing for her own brand Isak. She studied design in Sweden, Denmark and Chile and settled in the UK after extensive travelling, where she started up her business, combining the influences of those years of travelling and studying with her Scandinavian heritage.

Top / Bird
Cute birds inhabit a shapely tree in this fun design which was used on a birchwood tray.

Bottom / 1-20 Poster
The aim of this design was to create a nursery poster to help children learn to count. All shapes and sizes of birds have been illustrated using a sophisticated colour palette.

Opposite top left & Right /
Animals 1, Animals 2
Sandra loves to design and illustrate children's books. The criss-crossing patterns give the designs depth and style.

Middle left / Daisy
Middle right / Apple
In these two patterns Sandra shows her natural understanding of the pared-down aesthetic of Swedish design.

Bottom left /
Bookbinder's Design
The delicate, spiky flowers of this design are given extra dimension adding layers of texture.

Bottom right / Tulip
Strong, graphic shapes were used to create this design and the subtle blending of colour creates the shading to give it more depth.

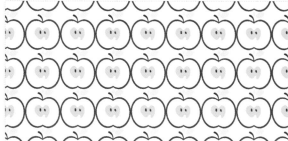

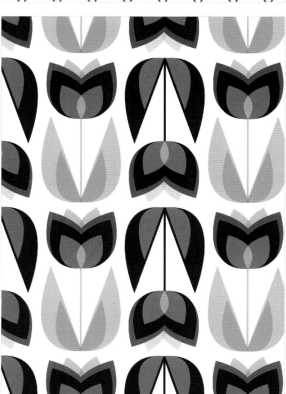

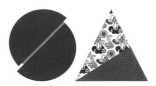

Sanna Annukka

www.sanna-annukka.com
www.bigactive.com/illustration/
sanna-annukka
info@sanna-annukka.com

102 // Sanna Annukka is a half-Finnish, half-English illustrator and printmaker with a love of nature and folklore. Having spent her childhood summers in the nightless Lapland wilderness, the forests, lakes and wildlife of the region have formed and infused her work. In 2006 her work was spotted by the British group Keane, which led to a very memorable collaboration on their second million-selling album, *Under the Iron Sea*. She has since been focusing on the development of a whole range of limited editions and other products for her own online shop, as well as becoming a new designer for leading Finnish textile and clothing company, Marimekko.

Above / Menagerie of Birds
This screen-print design expresses Sanna's love for birds.

Opposite top / Maidens
This design is also inspired by *The Kalevala* and a love of traditional folk costumes. Sanna is currently working on a complex print that will feature many maidens in traditional world costumes, varying from Saami folk costumes to African tribal wear.

Opposite bottom / Audubon's Aviary
A pattern designed for Japanese company Medicom Toy, to be applied to a range of textile products. Birds feature heavily in Sanna's work, so she especially enjoyed creating an entire pattern out of colourful bird characters.

Opposite / Midnight Sun
and Midnight Sun Birds
This personal work is based
on a dream Sanna had.

Top / Angry Owlets
Sanna loves owls and draws
them constantly. She enjoys
simplifying animals and
birds into series of shapes
and pattern.

Bottom / Pouches
These pouches are part of the
Audubon's Aviary product range
produced by Medicom Toy.

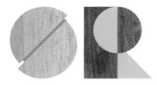

Scott Rhodes

www.scottrhodes.net
www.scottrhodesillustrator.blogspot.com
scott@scottrhodes.net

103 // Scott Rhodes is a freelance illustrator based in Chorlton, Manchester, who trained in illustration at Manchester Metropolitan University. In the 1990s Scott was a freelance traditional illustrator, painting designs for an independent card company and creating illustrations for packaging. By the turn of the century he'd converted to digital and the Apple Mac. Scott became freelance again in 2006 after working in design studios and now works in the fields of greetings card and wrapping paper design, editorial, advertising and publishing.

Top / Fawn Wood
An elegant fawn is created out of a wooden texture for a natural effect. This range was partly inspired by the wooden wallpaper in Scott's parents' house in the '70s.

Bottom / Norwegian Wood
This card was partly inspired by *Birch Forest* by Gustav Klimt. Published by Madison Park Greetings. The white trees look striking against the wooden ground.

Top left / Faux Bois Floral
Top right / Faux Bois Tree
The French *faux bois* translates as 'fake wood'. The design reflects the 'natural' look and nature is always an inspiration for Scott. The colourful, modern flowers and frilly border give these cards a feminine look.

Middle left / A is for Apples
Middle right / I Love Nature
Repeat pattern is used for these two greetings cards designs. They have a subtle hue thanks to the graph paper background which is allowed to show through the semi-transparent motifs. The Apples design was purchased by Tigerprint for Marks & Spencer.

Bottom left / Hi Cutie!
Scott loves to create cute characters, and these two are especially stylish.

Bottom right / Sweet Apples
Inspired by Japanese character art, the smiling apples are enhanced by the sweet multi-coloured, hand-drawn type.

Sean Sims

www.newdivision.com
claire@newdivision.com

104 // Originally from Middlesbrough, illustrator Sean Sims now lives in Brighton, where he juggles his work with looking after his two young children, Stanley and Mabel, which invariably means working bleary-eyed at night when they are tucked up in bed. Sean usually gets commissioned as an editorial illustrator, but is branching out more into surface patterns and other areas. He is inspired by children's book illustrators, such as Alain Grée, Miroslav Sasek and Charley Harper. Sean also has a large collection of design and decorative 'tat' from the '50s to the '70s.

Top / Valentine
A modern take on a traditional Valentine's theme featuring stylised birds with hearts. The serrated edge adds a nice touch.

Bottom / Sussex Detail
Opposite top / Sussex Village Pattern
A colourful and playful style makes these depictions of English village architecture so appealing.

Opposite bottom / Birdlife
Elegant birds and trees are arranged in a linear repeat, the pattern shows how a dark background can change a design from the more natural to the dramatic.

Overleaf left / Butterflies
The butterflies in this pattern are reduced to their very essence to become just two geometric shapes and a line, yet they remain recognisable.

Overleaf right / Fruit Pattern
A palette of citrus colours and loosely-shaped fruits make for a fun print.

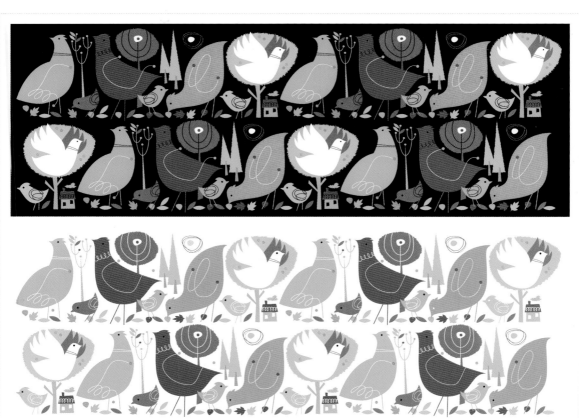

Sei

www.shopsei.com
info@shopsei.com

105 // Sei is a scrapbook company located in Logan, Utah, with graphic designers working in-house at their on-site art department. Sei has been able to serve as a training ground for the students at Utah State University. Their designers start working there part-time as students – learning about product development, packaging and design elements – and upon graduation move to full-time. Sei mainly sell to independent scrapbooking stores and craft stores, and have an independent store on-site.

Above / Tarragon
An elegant, leafy print, with hand-drawn strokes designed for a 30.5 x 30.5cm (12in x 12in) paper from the Dill Blossom collection.

Opposite / Coriander
A variety of naive, spiky seedheads in earthy tones, designed for a 30.5 x 30.5cm (12in x 12in) paper from the Dill Blossom collection.

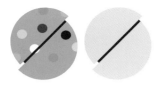

Showler and Showler

www.showlerandshowler.com
studio@showlerandshowler.com

106 // Showler and Showler is a collaboration between designers Hannah and Tom Showler, who both studied at the University of Brighton. They offer illustration and graphics services and also design cards and canvases under their own name, available to buy via their website and in various independent gift shops.

Top / Cakes
The paper cases are the consistent component in this pattern while the variety comes from the colours and shapes of the toppings. Created for a canvas.

Bottom / Love Cake
Originally designed as a greetings card then used as a mug design. Created with Valentine's or weddings in mind, the pattern and palette is romantic in feeling.

Opposite top / S and S Mugs
The mugs were a set of six commissioned by McLaggan Smith, and are based on original designs for greetings cards. The sweet, sugary pastel colours fit perfectly with the subject matter.

Opposite bottom left /
Doves Blue

Opposite bottom right /
Doves Pink
This design is used for a number of applications including mugs, cards and canvases. The doves are simply drawn and the freehand script adds a light touch.

Overleaf / Lollies
The variety in the shapes
and colours of ice lollies are
used to great effect in this
pastel-coloured, nostalgic
design created for
a greetings card.

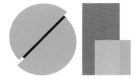

Silkie Lloyd

www.rosehipcards.co.uk
silkie@rosehipcards.co.uk

107 // Silkie Lloyd is a designer
based in Bristol, who studied
illustration and photography at
Bath Spa University. In 2004 Silkie
launched Rosehip, a stationery
and greetings publishing company,
selling to shops in the UK, Europe
and Australia. She also works freelance
doing surface pattern design for
interior and homeware collections.

Top & Opposite top left /
Brown Bird/Green Bird
Silkie's self-initiated project for
her own stationery range was
created using a combination
of hand-drawn images and
Illustrator, and inspired by
Jacobean crewel-work and the
Arts and Crafts movement.
Printed on 100 per cent
recycled wrapping paper
and notebooks.

Top right & Below left /
Stem Print 1 and 2
Inspired by vintage
Scandinavian design, these
patterns, used as covers
for Silkie's notebooks, were
designed using Illustrator.

Sophie Dupasquier

www.sophieillustration.co.uk
www.curlykale.com
sophie@dupasquier.co.uk

108 //   Sophie Dupasquier is a freelance illustrator and designer based in Brighton. She graduated in 2006 with a degree in illustration from Kingston University. Sophie works mainly for the editorial and publishing sectors, but also designs for her own small, family-run childrenswear company called CurlyKale, whose t-shirts, underwear and accessories can be bought online and in a few selected shops around the UK. Sophie is also a member of the illustration collective Candeo, along with two other illustrators from Kingston University, who love to get together to share ideas and organize exhibitions and fairs to promote and sell their work.

Top / Mousie
Created for CurlyKale childrenswear, this simple, girly and fun design could be applied to many different items, from pyjamas to pencil cases. The character was picked up from an old sketchbook doodle, then coloured in digitally and multiplied in Photoshop.

Bottom / Yellow Birdie
With a certain farmyard quality about it, this is a personal piece inspired by flocks of birds that gather to feed. Sophie likes to slightly off-register the colour layer to give a screen-printed look.

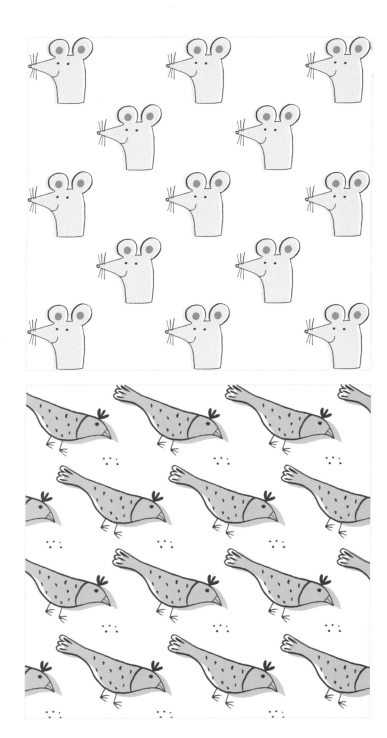

Above / Grey Elephant
This pattern was created for
CurlyKale childrenswear as a
simple, unisex design. Sophie's
patterns are often geared
towards young children, and
stem from funny characters
from her sketchbook.

Studio MIKMIK

www.studiomikmik.co.uk
www.studiomikmik.etsy.com
hello@studiomikmik.co.uk

109 // Studio MIKMIK was established in 2006 by graphic designer and illustrator Michael Lewis. Michael worked for several years in busy design studios before going freelance and setting up as Studio MIKMIK. Today he divides his time happily between design for print, illustration and personal projects including various screenprints and handcrafted paper products available through his Etsy shop.

Top / Vintage
Autumn Notebooks
Created from a printers over-run of wedding invitations these handmade notebooks are Japanese bound, made entirely from recycled paper and board and were printed using vegetable oil-based inks. The various stalks and leaves have a sophisticated look and are interspersed with dots and mushrooms.

Middle / Mushi Mushi
Below / Mini Mandalas
Bottom / Somewhere
Created as little mini icons these motifs are perfectly suited to badges. Printed using just two colours on a gocco printer.

Studio MIKMIK
Gocco Printed 25mm Badges

SOMEWHERE

Hello

Studio MIKMIK
Gocco Printed 25mm Badges

MUSHI MUSHI

Studio MIKMIK
Gocco Printed 25mm Badges

MINI MANDALAS

Top / Studio MIKMIK
Business Card
A smart bird and blossom
design in striking blue set
against a dark ground. Printed
on a super-heavy 350gsm FSC
card, as an extra special touch
the falling blossom petals
were picked out in varnish.

Below left / Mushi Mushi
Cute mushroom characters are
brought to life in this textured
two-colour A6 gocco print.
The funky typography makes
for a very distinctive look.

Below right / Badge Labels
Created as packaging for the
Studio Mik Mik badges these
designs echo those in the
pack. Michael's clean graphic
style is evident in the layout.

Sukie

www.sukie.co.uk
darrell@sukie.co.uk

110 // Sukie was founded in 2000 by Darrell and Julia Gibbs, after Darrell graduated from the Royal College of Art. Now based in Brighton, Sukie has gone on to design and produce a range of notebooks, accessories and home furnishings for their own brand, as well as working with fashion labels and international brands and on animation and illustration and design projects. They take great care in their choice of materials and now use recycled paper and organic cotton.

Top / Alphabet
The pattern on this cushion mixes old and made-up fonts, which have been screen-printed onto 100 per cent cotton.

Bottom / Junior Travel Journal
Featuring cats on mopeds, this journal has sewn-in storage pockets and colourful tear-off postcards.

Opposite / Patterned Bird Bag
This motif is influenced by '60s Scandinavian graphics.

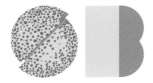

Susan Benarcik

www.susanbenarcik.com
susan@susanbenarcik.com

III // Susan Benarcik is an installation artist and surface designer based in New York City. Part printmaker and part sculptor, Susan's pattern designs and earth-inspired colour palette reflect her concern for the environment and love of natural materials. These designs are applicable to a variety of products, including stationery and printed and woven fabrics for home and fashion.

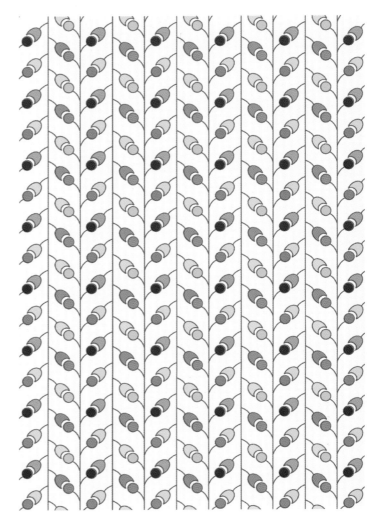

Top / Sol
This piece was designed in collaboration with fellow artist, Maria Cabo as an ongoing and experimental print collaborative. Using elemental forms from the natural world, they are transformed into an evocative pattern.

Opposite / Sea Forms
Original drawings taken from Susan's sketchbook were scanned, coloured and placed into repeat. Her love of nature is reflected in the earth-inspired colour palette, and the tiny dots make for a distinctive, softer design.

Susie Ghahremani

www.boygirlparty.com

112 // Susie Ghahremani graduated from the Rhode Island School of Design with a BFA in illustration, and has since received a number of art awards. Her artwork combines her love of nature, animals, music and patterns and has appeared in newspapers, books, magazines and advertising campaigns. In addition to painting, Susie also crafts her own line of products incorporating her original illustrations onto stationery, apparel, jewellery and other goodies, which can be found on her website.

Top / Song and Dance
Modestly sized but highly detailed this illustration created for a San Francisco art show features musical birds in a domestic setting. The wallpaper and flooring gives Susie the chance to show her love of pattern.

Bottom / Owl Buttons
Susie has added her illustrations to a host of interesting products, like these pin badges. Owls are a popular feature in her work, and these are filled with whimsical and delicate detail.

Opposite / Triangle in the Treetops
This art print was created for one of Susie's art show collections, Musical Chairs, involving anthropomorphized musical animals and quilt-like patterned backgrounds.

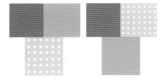

TamTam Design Studio

www.tamtamdesign.com
contact@tamtamdesign.com

113 // Tami Rasmussen, owner and designer at TamTam Design Studio, creates stylish, high-quality greetings cards and stationery products that utilize environmentally friendly materials and processes. Each card is hand assembled in the Chicago studio and printed on recycled papers using soy-based inks, and can be bought online as well as in select retail locations and boutiques across the US.

Top / Thanks So Very Much
A pretty card that captures the beauty of butterflies in flight thanks to the animated dotted lines.

Bottom / Congratulations Bouquet
Bouquet Inspired by wedding bouquets this simple illustration keeps a light and airy feel. The pattern on the left adds detail without dominating the main card.

Top left / I Love You, Mom
A bird with a chick in the nest is a great way to represent parenthood. The stylised tree shape acts as a great anchor on which to layout the design.

Top right / Cherry Blossom Friend
The Japanese influence is obvious in this design and colour scheme, but the style is fresh and modern.

Bottom / Thanks a Bunch
Delicate straight-lined flowers are placed beneath a simple, typographic embellishment.

TC Design

www.tcdesign.co.uk
info@tcdesign.co.uk

114 // TC Design is a publishing house based in Manchester and run by Tracy Webster. Tracy gained a BA (Hons) in Surface Pattern and Textiles at Bretton Hall, Leeds. After graduating she was lucky enough to be involved in a number of freelance projects that gave her the taste for greeting cards, and in 2003 TC Design was born. TC now has 14 greetings card ranges and also creates exclusive ranges, as well as taking on licensing and design commissions. Tracy has always been inspired by the things she sees around her, and is particularly influenced by Mid-century Modern ceramics and tableware, Scandinavian design, folk art, Lucienne Day and Charley Harper.

Top & Bottom / Seventies Child 'For the Seventies Child' card range. Tracy wanted to create an all-over pattern feel, and pushed this idea to incorporate shapes and symbols, such as the bird and apple.

Opposite top left & right / Dotty Dotty The use of black has proved very popular for TC Design, and this motif was inspired by the patterns used in children's annuals and television programmes from the '60s.

Opposite below left / Home Sweet Home From the 'Happy Occasions' range, this design is by Clare Birtwhistle. A repeat pattern of graphic houses separated by trees makes for a very modern take on a traditional theme.

Opposite middle right, bottom left & bottom right / Hello Petal This range of greetings cards was inspired by the designers of the '50s, '60s and '70s. Tracy likes to use simple shapes to create her patterns. Her love for all things vintage – and in particular vintage tablecloth patterns – has always been an inspiration and starting point, key to Tracy's design work and designing process.

new home

Congratulations

Ted & Rose

www.ted-and-rose.com
vartan@ted-and-rose.com

115 // Vartan Tekneyan is a
freelance designer based in Munich.
Vartan designs patterns under the
name Ted & Rose, and creates wall
art canvases that he sells online,
and at DaWanda. He also produces
custom-order prints for artists,
photographers, art gallery exhibitions
and interior designers.

Top / Little Orbits on Blue
Designed for wallpapers and
wall decoration, this layout
came about when Vartan
experimented with dashed lines.

Bottom / Seventies
Flowers Orange
A design for wallpaper and
fine-art prints on canvas that
was inspired by wallpapers
of the '70s.

Opposite top / Dots on a String
Vartan took inspiration for this
pattern from a large crowd of
birds sitting on a high-
voltage line.

Opposite bottom / Candy
Coloured Flowers
This layout for wrapping paper,
fabric and notebook covers
was inspired by the colours of
yoghurt gums, a kind of sweet.

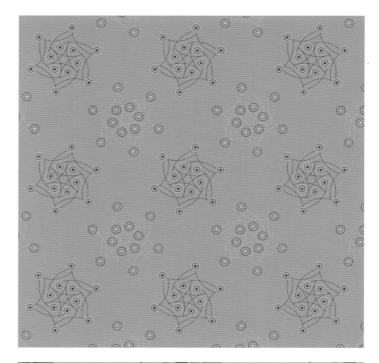

The Strawberry Card Company

www.thestrawberrycardcompany.co.uk
www.tsccillustration.co.uk
sian@thestrawberrycardcompany.co.uk

116 // The Strawberry Card Company is the work of designer Sian O'Donnell, who graduated from Plymouth University with a degree in art history with visual arts, and now works from her home in east Devon. Besides her card company, Sian also runs a new design business, TSCC Illustration, for all her licensing and commissions. She says "I love producing cards as it makes great design affordable and available to everyone."

Top / Pop Vintage Flowers
In this design the '60s pop culture merges beautifully with '50s cute polka dots and candy stripes.

Bottom / Pop Vintage Congratulations
Here traditional folk barge paintings are combined with '60s pop motifs.

Opposite top left /
Big Flowers Green
The Big Flowers range has a nostalgic feel, with muted colours and bold shapes for a very retro look.

Opposite top right /
Big Flowers Blue
Fabric and ceramic prints of the '50s and '60s were a huge inspiration for the Big Flowers range.

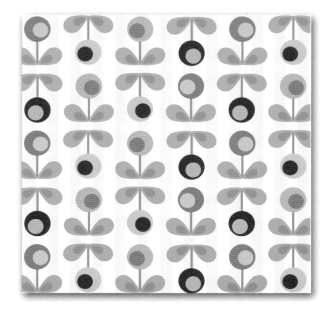

Opposite middle left /
Flora Red and Orange
The simple use of coordinating colours is what makes this design eye-catching.

Opposite middle right /
Flora Multicoloured
The bright colours and retro flowers of the Flora range are inspired by fabric prints of the '60s and '70s.

Bottom left / Bloom
Home Sweet Home
These houses are based on those in Sian's own street.

Bottom right / Bloom Love
This design was inspired by a classic nautical tattoo, creating a pretty design without being too girly.

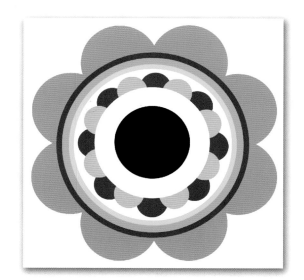

HOME SWEET HOME

LOVE

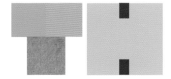

Tinee Kleinschroth

www.7morgen.blogspot.com
tinee@mytaikong.com

117 // Tinee Kleinschroth gained a degree in Fine Arts in 2001, and now lives and works as a freelance artist in Stuttgart. Tinee mainly concentrates on printmaking, but also works with illustration, paintings and collages. In 2007 Tinee created the label SiebenMorgen and opened her online shops on Etsy and DaWanda, selling original linocut prints and hand-printed paper goods, all produced in her printmaking studio.

Top / Peepz!
The mini-print series was created to make small artworks that are affordable to everybody. The layers of stamps are built up to create a woodland scene, and the natural course of the stamp running out of ink is used to great effect on the lettering.

Bottom / Tschilp!
Tschilp is the German word for 'chirp', and birds are a major theme in Tinee's work. This one was printed with a hand-cut rubber stamp made from Tinee's own drawing.

Opposite top / Daheim
This postcard set was hand printed on fine Dutch cardstock and paper, using hand-cut stamps of Tinee's own design. Each little house and line was printed separately in a different colour.

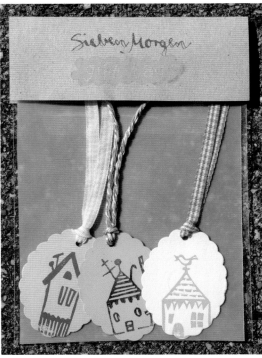

Bottom left / Home
Hand-printed and hand-cut in the SiebenMorgen printing
studio, these gift tags have a homespun charm. Little details
like the weather vanes and aerials create interest.

Bottom right / Note!
A hand-cut stamp from Tinees's own design, printed with
pigment ink on a little Muji notepad. Clever use is made
of a speech bubble, and the fox adds a quirky element.

We Are Family

www.wearefamilydesign.co.uk
info@wearefamilydesign.co.uk

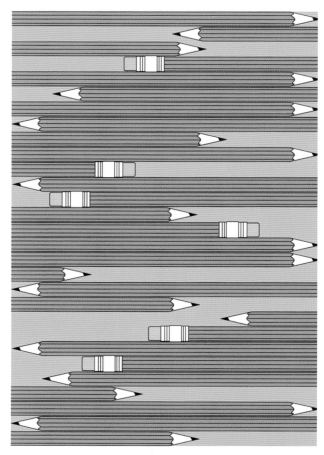

118 //   The We Are Family label was set up by Laura Coley, a graphic design graduate from Central Saint Martins who has gained a wide range of experience through working in some of London's most highly regarded design agencies. She also likes to draw, and her linear drawing style, love of pattern and fondness for bright, vibrant colour has spawned a cute and quirky greetings card range. The cards, printed in Britain using vegetable-based inks and high-quality FSC-certified stock, can be found in a number of prestigious shops and galleries in the UK. In addition to the We Are Family products, Laura continues to work as a freelance graphic designer.

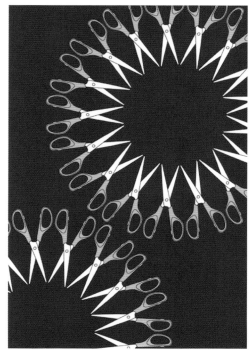

Top / Pencils
This simple pencil design is great for thank-you cards or sending to particularly arty friends.

Bottom / Scissors
From this everyday object comes a decorative starburst or graphic flower pattern.

Opposite / Keys
This card is designed to be sent in celebration of moving house, but could equally be used to congratulate someone on passing their driving test or on their 21st birthday.

Overleaf left / Crackers
This bright red festive cracker card is one of the more traditional designs in the Christmas Dinner series.

Overleaf right / Sprouts
An homage to the humble sprout, this card was designed to be sent at Christmas.

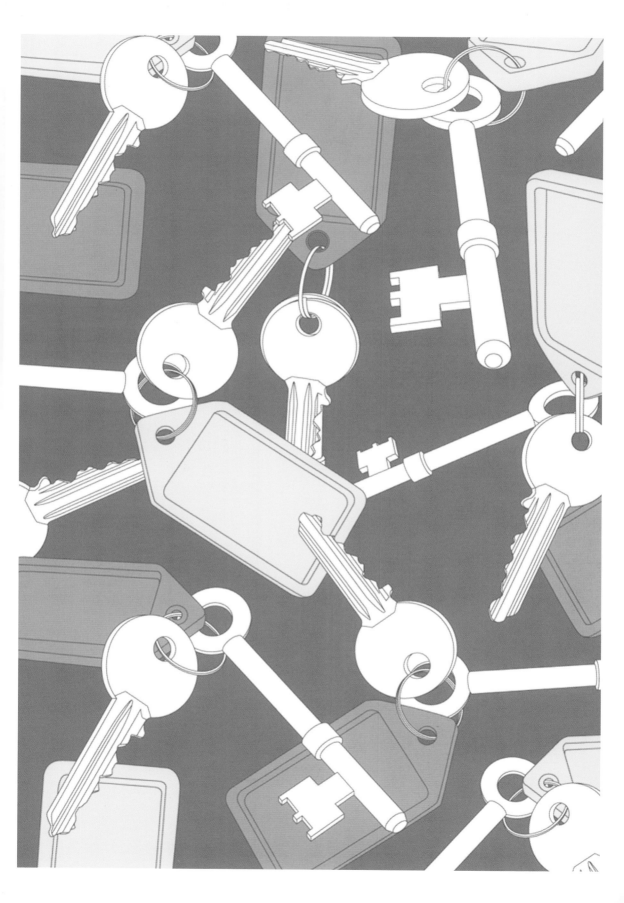

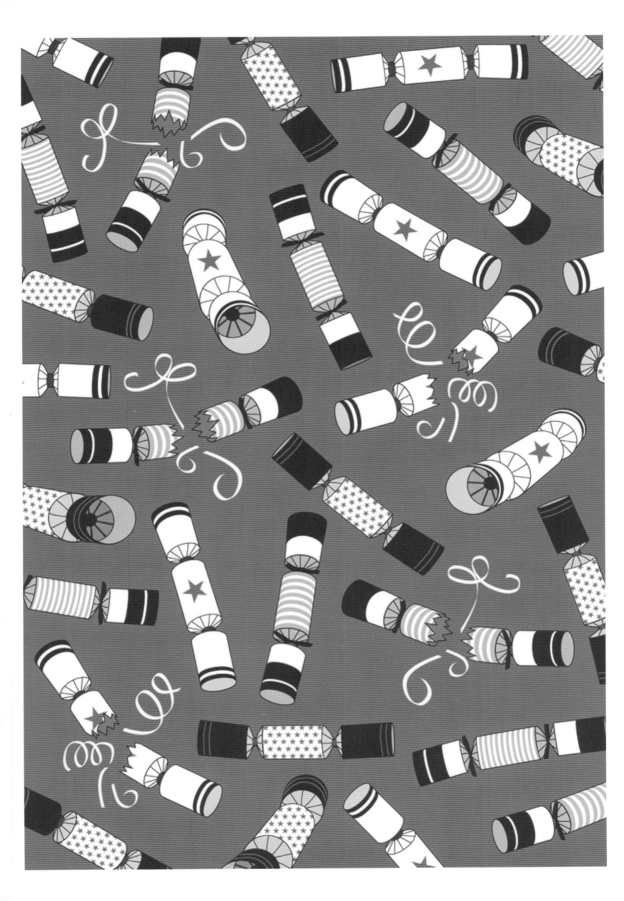

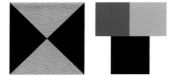

Xenia Taler

www.xeniataler.com
info@xeniataler.com

119 //   The ceramic company Xenia Taler is primarily known for its tiles, but also produces other ceramic products such as picture frames, vases and boxes. Their products are sold in shops and galleries throughout North America and from their own website. Xenia's art tiles are used as wall hangings and trivets, but they also produce tiles suitable for permanent grouted installations. All items are produced in their studio in Toronto.

    Xenia Taler is the artist responsible for the illustrations, and the ceramic images are made possible by her partner Steven Koblinsky, through his knowledge of ceramic processes and glazes. Recently their designs have also been licensed and used in the creation of other products, such as greetings cards and journals.

Above / Crochet Tree
Xenia wanted to make a lacy, delicate design for this tile, part of a larger series that includes a peacock, butterflies, doves and two 'rustic' folk.

Opposite / Blossom Tail
This tile design is now being licensed for a notebook and a card produced by Barnes & Noble. An abstracted flower head provides a dramatic motif and the low-contrast blues sit perfectly with the neutral colour of the background.

Yuyu

www.iloveyuyu.com
hello@iloveyuyu.com

120 // Yuyu is a Leeds-based, design-led publisher of greetings cards, wrapping papers and social stationery. The people behind Yuyu are Mark McKeown and Julie Hughes, both designers but with diverse backgrounds. Julie has over 12 years of experience in fashion textile and surface pattern design, and has worked for studios in New York and London. Mark has over 15 years of experience in graphic and editorial design. They met four years ago, and since then Julie's passion for surface pattern and print has started to influence Mark's everyday graphic design work. In 2007 they decided to combine their different skills to create Yuyu, and launched their first collection in July 2008.

Above / Bloom 07
For this design Julie's
Scandinavian-inspired
sketches were brought
to Illustrator and redrawn
using a graphics tablet.

Left / Bloom 08
A limited colour palette
featuring just a handful of
bright, vivid hues, combined
with exotic floral shapes and
bold, geometric patterns,
creates a striking and
unique style.

Acknowledgements

I would love to thank:
all the designers and illustrators who
gave their work to create this book;
the readers and sponsors of the Print
& Pattern website who have helped
it grow; Helen Evans for recognising
the need for a book of this kind and
for allowing me the total freedom to
curate it; Peter Jones for guiding it
into creation; & SMITH for their
fantastic layouts and typography.
Thanks to Mum, Dad, Mark, and Lisa
for all their support and encouragement.

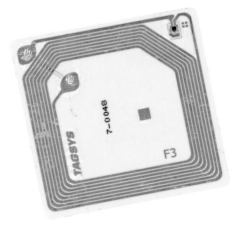